On My Way to BALTIMORE

Linda Thielfoldt

American Quilter's Society
www.AmericanQuilter.com

The American Quilter's Society or AQS is dedicated to quilting excellence. AQS promotes the triumphs of today's quilter, while remaining dedicated to the quilting tradition. We believe in the promotion of this art and craft through AQS Publishing and AQS QuiltWeek®.

CONTENT EDITOR: CAITLIN RIDINGS
GRAPHIC DESIGN: ELAINE WILSON
COVER DESIGN: MICHAEL BUCKINGHAM
HOW-TO PHOTOGRAPHY: LINDA THIELFOLDT
QUILT PHOTOGRAPHY: CHARLES R. LYNCH
ASSISTANT EDITOR: ADRIANA FITCH
DIRECTOR OF PUBLICATIONS: KIMBERLY HOLLAND TETREV

Additional copies of this book may be ordered from the American Quilter's Society, PO Box 3290, Paducah, KY 42002-3290, or online at www.ShopAQS.com.

Attention Photocopying Service: Please note the following—Publisher and author give permission to print pages 66 and 82–93.

American Quilter's Society
www.AmericanQuilter.com

Library of Congress Cataloging-in-Publication Data

PENDING

COVER: TULIP SPLENDOR, full quilt, p. 51.
TITLE PAGE: NOTTINGHAM POMEGRANATE, full quilt, p. 63.
RIGHT: MARYLAND ROSE, full quilt, p. 44.

Dedication

· · · · · · · · · · · · ·

With love and a grateful heart I say thank you to my biggest cheerleader and fan, my best friend and person I love most in the world, my husband Devan. Thank you for giving me encouragement and room to create. You are as much a part of my quilting adventures as I am. Thank you from the bottom of my heart.

This book would not have been possible without the help and encouragement of my two best friends and partners in quilting crime, Janet Rose and Karen Lieberman. Thank you for your contribution and help with this book. Also, for being ready and willing to come alongside wherever this quilting journey has taken me. You both have my heart and I thank you for sharing your mad quilting skills with me.

Lastly, but certainly not least, I thank God for giving me a mother who taught me to sew and never once put boundaries on me. She opened up a whole world to me when she shared her excellent sewing skills with me. I love you Mom and I'll see you again one day.

COLOSSIANS 3:12 …*clothe yourselves with compassion, kindness, humility, gentleness and patience.*

Acknowledgments

· · · · · · · · · · ·

To quilters everywhere and especially you, the person who bought this book, I say a huge thank you. Your thirst for learning and growing is what inspires me. I do hope you enjoy this book and make wonderful things. If you make a quilt from this book or use some of the designs in your own creative way please email me a photo, I would love to see what you create!

Thanks to my students who validate my skills, talent, and make me reach ever higher. I hope I have, in some small way, inspired you as much as you have inspired me.

Thank you to AQS, especially my editorial and graphics team, who made my job and the process of writing this book so much easier.

Blessings,

Linda

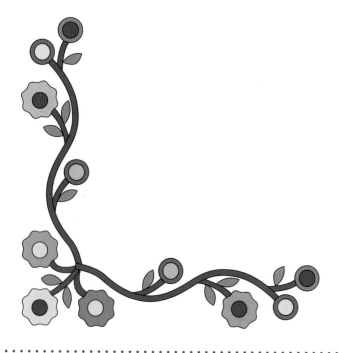

Contents

Introduction

· · · · · · · · · · · ·

The Beginning

It was love at first sight the day I saw an antique Baltimore Album quilt up close and personal. I was in awe. I was an intermediate quilter and at that moment knew that I would never make one. I had a family and a career, and the time and skills it would take to make a true Baltimore Album quilt were out of my grasp. To this day I still love them and yet, to this day I know I will never make one. That my friend is how this book came to be, I love the traditional appliqué blocks of the 19th century but I live in the 21st century and don't have the time to invest in a "real" Baltimore Album quilt. So with this book you can enjoy some of the aesthetics of Baltimore Album quilts without having to make such a huge investment in time to make one.

Appliqué has been a passion of mine for many years. There are many methods and I feel I have tried them all. I've come to the point in my quiltmaking where I do mostly machine work and all the quilts in this book were made using the buttonhole stitch feature of my sewing machine along with fusible web. If you have never tried this method, I encourage you to do so. It's quick and yields great results. However, all of the block designs are suitable for any appliqué method you choose and if you are a lover of handwork the pieces are mostly large and easy to needle turn. All of the quilts have pieced borders or elements that really add to the quilt and while they are not traditional Baltimore Album quilt elements, I think they add so much to the quilts. I've incorporated string piecing into one of the quilts and if you have never tried it I encourage you to do so, it allows you to add a bunch of colors and fabrics and is just a whole lot of fun!

OPPOSITE: SEVILLE, full quilt, p. 70

· ·

The Concept of the Book

In my quest to make the appliqué the focus of every quilt and yet at the same time, doable for the average quilter, I decided bigger was better. I also added in some pieced elements not typical of Baltimore Album quilts and I think they really help mix things up.

Most of the Baltimore Album quilts I have seen over the years have been based on a 12" finished block size. Most of the projects in the book are based on a common finished block size of 18" which allows you to complete a quilt in less time and mix and match the appliqué designs within most of the quilts in the book. In addition to the larger size, the quilts feature pieced elements that are usually quicker to complete than traditional appliqué and often add an interesting element to each quilt. There are 19 different block designs in the book and they can be mixed and matched to fit your personal preference. All but two of the quilts in the book show the same quilt in a completely different colorway which may give you an idea of how color and fabric can really change the look of any quilt.

Baltimore Album quilts are dramatic due to their intricacy and colors and in order to get that same sense of drama I have upsized the designs and used fabrics and colors of today and yet with a nod to the quilts of the 1800s. Come join me as we take this journey *On Our Way to Baltimore*.

Tools and Supplies

· · · · · · · · · · · ·

Fabric

Lots of pretty fabric! This for me is where the fun begins and I love choosing fabrics for a new quilt. The projects in this book feature a wide range of fabrics, some reproductions, some moderns, some contemporary floral, plenty of tone-on-tone prints that read as a solid, and just about everything else except batiks and flannels. There is no limit.

Students often tell me that choosing fabrics is the hardest part. They don't know where to start. One of my favorite ways to choose fabrics is to find a larger print that has a look and color I like and go from there. For example the red floral fabric I used in CARNIVALE (p. 76) is a lively print with lots of colors. I chose the colors for the quilt from the color palette used in the print. Even if the quilt you are making does not have a place for a traditional border you can still use a print with lots of colors as your starting point. If you find that you like the colors together in a particular fabric, chances are they will also look great together in a quilt. If you don't want to or if the layout does not allow for a larger print, it really is a great way to select fabrics.

Don't match your fabrics too much. You need some differences in value and tones.

Don't choose fabrics that blend too well, you need some spark. Often, that odd color that you don't think goes is just what the quilt needs. Don't be afraid to mix it up. Check out the alternate quilts for the projects in the book and see how choosing different fabrics give the designs a completely new look just from the color and style of the fabrics used in the quilt.

Sewing Machine

Get your machine ready to sew. Take out the bobbin case and clean any lint or dirt out of the chase. Check your bobbin case carefully, if your machine has one, as that is a great place for lint to hang out and it can mess with your tension. If you haven't installed a new needle in quite some time, do so now. If you are a seasoned quilter like me, you can tell when a needle is getting dull, as it makes a different sound as you sew. Some people like to change the needle with every new project. I don't, but needles are inexpensive and that may work for you. Bottom line: if you are sewing along and all of a sudden you start having issues with either the tension, skipped stitches, or thread breakage, it's time for a new needle. I use a 75/11 quilting needle in my machine when piecing or doing appliqué stitching.

Machine Feet

To me there are two feet that are worth the investment. An open toe appliqué foot and a ¼" piecing foot. If they are available for your machine they are worth every penny.

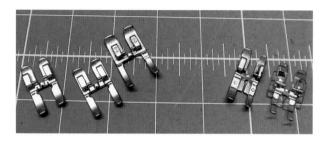

Fig. 1. Samples of open toe appliqué feet on the left and ¼" piecing feet on the right

Iron

This is an essential tool in the quiltmaking process. I no longer buy expensive irons that seem to need diapers after only a short while. I buy irons when on sale so when it starts to need a diaper, I don't feel the least bit guilty when I toss it in the recycle bin. Some people never use water so the diaper issue never comes up but for those of us who like a bit of steam this is a common problem. It is also a good idea to have some iron cleaner on hand when dealing with fusibles. You can usually find it in the housewares department and it comes in a tube. If you have an iron with a stainless steel soleplate you can also use my Mom's old trick – salt! Dump a Tablespoon or so of white table salt onto a stack of paper towels, place your hot iron on the paper towel over the salt and iron back and forth with no steam. This will usually remove any errant fusible and you can get right back to work. Be careful though, you can end up with salt everywhere.

Ironing Board

A good ironing board is almost as important as the iron. You don't want it too cushy, but rather a firm surface that does not move when you press. A good tip when using fusibles is to iron a large piece of freezer paper to your ironing board before you start. If you happen to get any fusible on your ironing board it is easy to just peel off the freezer paper so your ironing board cover stays nice and clean.

Appliqué Pressing Sheet

Worth every penny! There are lots of layers and pieces in many of the designs in this book and in the building units or parts of the design. Fusing them together before you fuse the complete motif to the base fabric is very helpful. I use mine constantly and if you have never used one I highly recommend purchasing one. Buy the largest one you can afford. Some people also have good luck with parchment paper but I have had mixed results. It's just not worth it to me to waste the time and money on fabric and fusible only to have to toss it and start over when I can't remove it from the parchment paper.

Scissors or Snips

You will need scissors to cut the paper fusible and then scissors or snips to cut the fabric after fusing. I prefer to use paper scissors for cutting the fusible shapes out, I figure the less wear and tear on my good scissors the better. I also am a big fan of the spring loaded snips for cutting the shapes because they cut down on hand fatigue.

General Quiltmaking Instructions

· · · · · · · · · · · ·

The information in this section provides the technical knowledge you need in order to appliqué and piece the projects in the book. Many of these are time-honored methods that you may already be aware of. If you have a favorite way of doing any of the steps in the quilts in this book, by all means use what you know or what works for you.

Fabric

The instructions assume that you will be using good quality quilting cotton with a 42" useable width of fabric. You may choose to prewash your fabrics but in my 40+ years of quiltmaking I have never done that and don't plan to start.

Many of the quilts are scrappy, made with fabrics pulled from my vast stash and as such, generous amounts are given for all yardage listed.

Rotary Cutting

Unless otherwise instructed, please cut all pieces across the width of fabric on the straight of grain. WOF is referred to in the patterns and it is an acronym for Width of Fabric.

Strips and Squares

Place your folded fabric on your cutting mat and take a large rectangular ruler and align a vertical line on the ruler exactly on the fold. Trim off the uneven end of the piece of fabric using the horizontal edge of the ruler and then start cutting the necessary strips or squares from that edge. If there are lots of strips to cut, I often re-check the fold and sometimes have to re-cut the bottom edge to keep things square. If you have ever gotten a V at the fold on a strip of fabric it is because the vertical line on the ruler was not exactly on the fold as you cut the strip.

Half-Square Triangles

Many of the designs in the projects call for half or quarter-square triangles. Take great care in cutting each square as the triangles are only as good as the square they start with.

To cut half-square triangles (HST) from a square, lay a ruler diagonally across the square, with the cutting edge exactly on the two (2) corners. Make the cut and afterwards, pull the triangles away before you move the ruler. That way, if your cutter didn't make it all the way through you can easily cut again (fig. 1, p. 12).

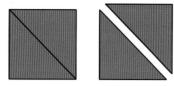

Fig. 1. Half-square triangles

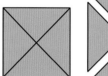

Fig. 2. Quarter-square triangles

The same procedure is used for quarter-square triangles but in addition to the first cut you pick up your ruler and cut again from the opposite two (2) corners (fig. 2).

Pinning

I recommend pinning the patchwork parts of the quilts. I pin at regular intervals and always use pins on all sewn seam intersections. I place a pin on either side of the matched up seam. In some cases where I have points coming together at a seam intersection I also put one pin across the seam perpendicular to the seam I'm sewing. I only use fine glass head silk pins. They are so thin that they don't

Designer Tip

If a project requires several half-square triangle units there is a quick and easy method whereby you make eight (8) HST units at one time. The formula works for any size HST unit you need to make. You take the size of the square you would normally use for making two (2) HSTs and just double that. For example, to make a pair of HSTs where the pattern calls for cutting two (2) squares of fabric that are 3⅞" x 3⅞" you just double the size of the starting square. So in this example you would cut two

(2) squares that are 7¾" x 7¾". You draw lines on the fabric square from corner to corner. Sew a ¼" seam on both sides of both lines. Then you cut the squares exactly in half. Then you cut again along both of the original drawn lines. What you will end up with is eight (8) HST units made from just two (2) squares of fabric. This method does not generally work as well if you are going for a totally scrappy look but is a huge timesaver if you are only working with two (2) fabrics and have a lot of HST units to make.

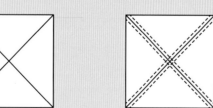 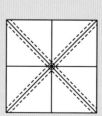 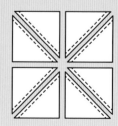

distort the fabric thereby causing things you thought you were matched up to not be after the seam is sewn.

Machine Piecing

Unless otherwise instructed, always join your fabric pieces with right sides together using a scant ¼" seam allowance. I find that a ¼" quilting foot is a must when doing precision piecing. If you don't have one you can take a stack of sticky notes and peel off an ⅛" or so stack of them and after finding your exact ¼" seam line on your machine adhere the stack next to your presser foot. The stack of sticky notes can then be used as a guide and won't harm your machine. On certain machines you have to move the needle toward the right to get in the correct position if using a normal presser foot. I find this problematic because I can be pretty sure I'm going to sew a bunch of pieces where I forgot to move the needle. This is why I'm a huge advocate of buying the ¼" foot – less hair pulling later!

Chain piecing is a huge timesaver and for projects with many pieces to be joined it is the way to sew. It saves thread which is a bonus. To chain piece, you simply feed your patchwork units through the machine one after another without snipping the threads or stopping (fig. 3). When you finish chain piecing, press as instructed in the pattern (usually to the dark), BEFORE you snip the threads in between each unit. This saves even more time handling multiple smaller pieces that need to be pressed.

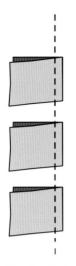

Fig. 3. Chain stitch piecing

Thread

Being a self-taught quilter I was not aware of the rules of quilting. You know all the things you MUST do in order to keep the Quilt Police at bay. The topic of thread in quilting is one that can be fraught with controversy and I'm sure many quilters would take issue with what I'm about to say. I piece with a very fine polyester thread. Before many of the thread manufacturers came out with fine poly threads I used a good quality serger thread. Not the stuff in the wire bin for $1 at the discount store! GASP! I know, I know, you have all heard the horror stories. I'm here to tell you that in over 40 years of quiltmaking, I have never had the thread rip, shred, destroy, or eat through the cotton quilt fabric. I like the thin thread because your piecing is more accurate. You don't lose as much from the "turn of the cloth." If you have ever cut accurately, then pieced, and pressed correctly with less than perfect results I would bet the thread is the culprit.

Bottom line: choose a thread you know, that your machine likes, and that works well for you. I am not a purist and many of the threads of today are a thousand times better than the threads of all the quilters that came before us. Don't be afraid to experiment.

Pressing

This is a key step in precision quiltmaking. I press throughout the whole piecing process and press each seam. I like to use a hot iron and steam. When I know I have gotten the desired results, I hit the pieces with a spritz of sizing and press again. Some prefer a dry iron. Others prefer a dry iron along with a pressing spray of some kind. Those methods are fine too. Choose the one that works the best for you and your iron. No matter the method, it is important to have a firm pressing surface.

Generally you place the dark fabric of a patchwork unit wrong side facing so you can see it. Take your iron and press along the seam line(s). You then lift the top fabric (dark) up and away from you and gently press the top piece away from you. Make sure the seam is well pressed without any fold or flap. Press the seam flat. At this point I like to give my pieces a shot of Magic® Sizing Fabric Finish spray for

Designer Tip

If you use the spray finish first and miss iron a piece, it is often difficult to get that seam/fold line that was incorrectly pressed out of the fabric so I always do it after I know I have the results I want.

a crisp finish. You don't want to totally wet the fabric, a fine mist will do.

Triangle units are used throughout this book and it is important that you press them properly. I lay the unit on my pressing surface and finger press them open after initially setting the seam as above. I like to get the fabric to behave a bit before I hit it with my iron. You are dealing with bias edges on HSTs and pressing them incorrectly can lead to many undesirable outcomes. Take your time.

Appliqué Methods

Before beginning your project please make note of the sizing requirements of the patterns you plan to use found on pp. 82–93 and make the appropriate copies. There are several methods for appliqué but all the quilts in this book were made using the buttonhole stitch on my machine along with a fusible web. It is known as raw edge appliqué. I have been using the same brand of fusible web since I started making appliqué quilts and those quilts have held up well when properly stitched down. Washing and drying multiple times has not resulted in frayed edges or caused the fabrics to lift away from the quilt. One trick I use that really helps is to match your appliqué thread to the color of the fabric you are stitching down. I find it less distracting than using a contrasting thread and many people are shocked to discover that my quilts are done using fusible raw edge appliqué. If none of the colors of thread you have match the fabric perfectly, I suggest going a tad darker. It will usually blend and hide better than if you choose a lighter thread.

I like to use a good quality cotton or polyester all-purpose thread for the buttonhole stitching. Some people like 100% cotton, and some like to use rayon, or embroidery thread. While that is fine and adds an element of shine and glitz, I don't feel the rayon thread is as durable over the long run. Experiment. The right choice of thread is the one that gives you the results you want and runs trouble free in your machine.

Know your machine. My machine has a feature that allows me to program any number of stitch combinations to get the results I want. This allows me to add an extra stitch or an extra buttonhole stitch at the beginning or the end of the normal stitch that is pre-programmed into my machine. Experiment with the stitches on your machine and try different widths and lengths. I personally like a smaller stitch both in width and length. The correct combination is the one you like and that your machine can do.

Designer Tip

Rarely is there a discussion about bobbin thread when it comes to machine appliqué. I use the same thread in the bobbin as I do for piecing. It is thinner thread. I just use a neutral color and loosen my top tension so that the top thread is pulled ever so slightly to the back of the quilt block. This way the bobbin thread never shows and I don't have to deal with multiple thread color changes in the bobbin.

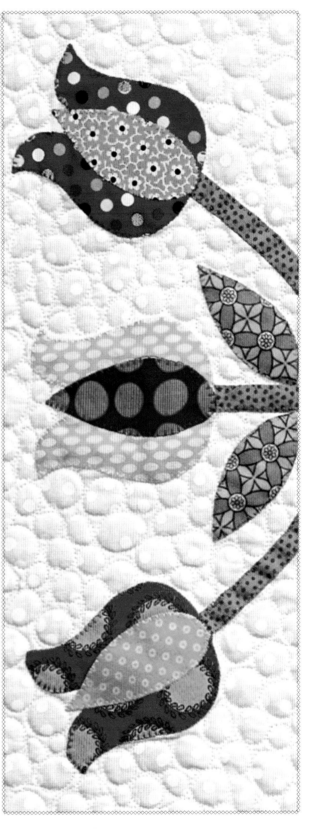

TULIP SPLENDOR, full quilt, p. 51.

When I have all the appliqué components fused in place I decide what area I want to buttonhole stitch first and then I do all the pieces in that color before I change threads. This means I may do all the green or all the red in all the blocks before I change threads. It streamlines the process, but you must do all the cutting and fusing of all the blocks in the quilt before you start sewing if you want to minimize thread changes.

Using Fusible Web

If you have never used fusible web for appliqué I urge you to purchase and try several different brands. I personally like Wonder Under® by Pellon®. It is reliable, easily found, inexpensive, and it's not fussy if you over iron like some other brands. Also, if you use the halo method, it does not leave the fabric feeling overly stiff. Follow the manufacturer's instructions being sure to place the fusible (usually rough) side down on the fabric. After fusing, cut out the pieces on the drawn line. I leave the backing on the fused shapes until right before I'm ready to fuse them down. If you cannot get the paper to peel away it is often helpful to score the paper with a pin and then peel away from that scored line.

Tracing the Pattern Pieces

Many of the designs have elements that need to over or underlap the piece adjacent to them. Be sure to add a little extra to what you are tracing to allow for this. This is most often the case with stems, I usually extend the lines about ¼" beyond what the pattern shows.

The Halo Method

This method, I believe, is the absolute best way to do fusible raw edge appliqué. You cut out your shapes that have been traced onto the fusible paper backing leaving about a ¼" around the outside of the drawn lines. After the pieces are cut you then cut inside the line also leaving about a ¼".

Pay attention to direction. Most of the appliqué patterns in the book are not directional. If you want a specific bird to appear on a particular side of the design for instance, be sure to draw the shape on the fusible in reverse if necessary. A light box is helpful in that instance.

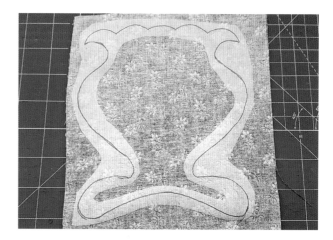

Fig. 4. Halo Method

> ## *Designer Tip*
>
> A non-stick appliqué pressing sheet is a wonderful tool when "building" your block designs. When dealing with multiple pieces I like to assemble the shapes as they appear in the quilt, laying them on top of one another as required. Then I fuse them to each other using the non-stick sheet before fusing them to the base block. This is especially helpful on some of the flowers that have multiple pieces.

Prepare Your Machine for Appliqué

It is important to really know your machine so a little practice is in order. I like to use my machines buttonhole appliqué stitch and you need to find a stitch width and length that you like and gives you the look you want. On my machine I use a 2.0 x 1.5, but I suggest you make a sample on light colored fabric of different combinations and mark the numbers on your sample. You then have a reference every time you start a new project and you don't have to try and remember the correct settings. Keep in mind that smaller pieces may require a small stitch length and width and it's OK to change the scale.

If your machine has a needle down feature, engage that, as it is very helpful when you have to pivot at corners or the points of leaves and other shapes. Guide the stitching with your hands resting lightly on the fabric. For curves, guide and turn the fabric as you continue sewing. I find I get better results if I stitch at a fairly fast pace only stopping to pivot. If the curve is dramatic you may need to release the presser foot a few times and make sure the needle is down to adjust the position of the fabric. Pay attention to where your needle rests at the stopping point. Sometimes it is helpful to make one more stitch to be certain the needle is on the correct side when you continue stitching, this is especially important at corners.

To help get to know your machine I suggest cutting and fusing several shapes – a square, a circle, a triangle, and a leaf. Stitch around each one to learn how your machine functions and what you need to do in order to hit the points you need to as you sew and turn the fabric.

If your machine does not have a buttonhole stitch you can experiment with some of the decorative stitches you may have or even just use the zigzag stitch. I have had students use a straight stitch along the edges with good results. Experiment and see what you prefer given the capabilities of your machine.

Using a locking or tie-off stitch to complete each appliqué stitching line provides security. My machine has this feature, but if your machine does not, just make three tiny stitches almost on top of one another. You do this by holding the fabric piece in one place and not allowing the feed dogs to advance the fabric. It may seem awkward at first but if you try it and practice a little you will soon get the hang of it. Additionally your machine may have a single stitch function and that can work well too. Doing this is also helpful when you have appliqué shapes that are in close proximity but you need to "jump" from one to the other. Doing the tie off and not trimming the thread between the different shapes cuts down on the time and thread. You just sew one shape, tie-off, and then jump over to the next and continue stitching. Thread tails can be trimmed later.

Completing the Quilt Top

Once all the components are together and the appliqué stitching is complete it is time to put the quilt top together. Each pattern within the book has specific instructions on the order of assembly. In general, you assemble the center of the quilt or blocks first. Take some time to evaluate placement and make any changes you need in order to have a pleasing layout. Having a large space to lay out all the components is really helpful. A design wall is a great addition to any sewing space.

Borders

Many quilters have specific rules about borders. How to cut them, what order to sew them onto the quilt, and probably a bunch of other rules I'm not aware of. When I first started quilting I didn't have a teacher and in those days quilting books were few and far between. In the beginning I would just cut my strips of border fabric and start sewing at one edge and continue on to the opposite edge. When I got to the end of the quilt I would just trim off the excess border fabric. Results were pretty good. Then someone told me you should measure the two (2) edges and also

the middle of the quilt and take an average of those three measurements and cut the border fabric to that length and then pin and ease or stretch the border fabric to fit the quilt top. I had mixed results with this method and I soon abandoned it. Over the past decade I have used what I think is just a logical way to figure out the length to cut the borders for all four (4) sides of the quilt. Just measure the edge. I know, it's a shock! I'm sure there are some of the quilt police on the hunt for me at this moment! I just apply logic to my border application process and I have won some nice quilt show awards using just this method. Once the borders are cut to the correct measurement it's imperative that you pin it to the quilt before sewing.

Backing

There are so many options for quilt backing these days. You can purchase extra wide fabric in all sorts of prints and solid colors. You can seam yardage to the appropriate size or you can do what I often do and that is use some of the leftover fabrics from the front to piece the backing to fit the quilt. Whichever method you choose be sure to allow some extra fabric all the way around the quilt. If you are having the quilt professionally quilted, most longarm quilters suggest 4"–6" on all sides. When I was quilting for customers I always appreciated that extra fabric.

Batting

There are so many choices when it comes to batting and a good place to start is to answer four questions:

How Do You Plan to Use the Quilt?

If the quilt is meant to be a quilt to snuggle under, one that will get lots of use, you may want to consider a natural fiber/poly blend. The blend will make the quilt soft, supple, and very easy to care for.

If the quilt is to be hung on a wall, look for a batting with scrim. Scrim will help the quilt hang straight and flat. I always use batting with scrim for my competition quilts.

If you are in a warm climate most of the time a silk or wool batting might be a good choice as both are natural fibers and less heavy/dense than cotton.

How Will the Quilt Be Quilted?

Most quilt battings on the market can be quilted with ease. You don't have to worry about how far apart they have to be quilted as much as you had to in the past. However, lots of dense quilting may impact how a batt performs. A thick felt-like batting will become very stiff with lots of quilting. Thinner battings are more challenging to use on a longarm and often cannot take the handling and tugging. Check with your longarm quilter to see if they have a preference. It's a good idea to take into consideration the amount of quilting you plan for on a quilt when choosing batting.

How Will the Quilt Be Cared For?

If you plan to wash your quilt, keep in mind that the batting will shrink unless it is 100% polyester. Some battings may felt (wool for example) and some of the new battings are air dry only. Please read the care labels before choosing a quilt batting. This is especially critical if your quilt will be a gift, I often include washing instructions on the label so the recipient knows how to care for a handmade quilt. If shrinkage is a concern then a poly blend such as an 80/20 is often a good choice.

Will the Batting Impact the Fabrics?

This is an important thing to consider. For example if you used mostly dark fabrics in your quilt you may want to consider a dark batting, there are many on the market. If you are concerned about bearding you should consider a batting that has been manufactured by bonding. My experience is that a resin bonded batting will beard less than a thermally bonded one. Needle punched battings will typically beard more than a bonded batting.

My best advice when choosing batting is to read the labels and do some testing.

Quilting

Many of the quilts of the nineteenth-century have some common quilting elements such as crosshatching, outlining of appliqué, feathers, plumes, leaf motifs, floral motifs, and other linear fill designs. As an avid machine quilter, I love adding these types of designs to my quilts. I also am a believer in stitching on the appliqué. You see that often in antique quilts and due to the size of many of the motifs in my quilts it is a necessity.

Many of the quilting designs used on the quilts in this book are my own freehand designs and there are no patterns for them. Several of the motif-based designs are for sale in both paper and digital formats.

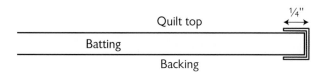

Fig. 5. Double layer French binding

Fig. 6. Cut binding strips 2" wide. Trim the ends of each of the 2" x WOF binding strips on a 45° angle

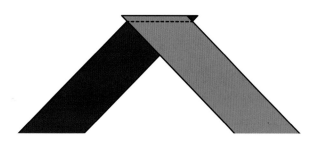

Fig. 7. Stitch the diagonal ends together using a ¼" seam allowance

Binding

Many quilters use strips cut 2½" wide for double French-fold binding. I'm not a fan of that size and prefer to use a strip cut 2" wide for all my binding which gives me a finished width of between ¼" and ⁵⁄₁₆". Experiment with different sizes and see what you prefer. I always cut enough strips so that I have at least 15" in length beyond what I need for any given quilt. I never use a single fold binding as I want the binding to last as long as the quilt. If the quilt has a serpentine edge you must cut your binding fabric on the bias.

Trim the ends of each of the 2" x WOF binding strips on a 45° angle.

Piece the binding strips together and press the seams open. Press the binding in half lengthwise to make a binding that measures 1" wide. Attach to the quilt using your preferred method using a ¼" seam.

> **Note**
> A 2" wide strip makes approximately ⁵⁄₁₆" wide finished binding. Adjust the size of the strip to your preferred size if you like.

Hanging Sleeve

Many of my quilts are for competition. I almost always attach a hanging sleeve to quilts, unless I know the quilt is meant to snuggle under. I cut strips 10" wide x WOF and sew together enough strips to go across the side of the quilt it will hang from. I then serge a seam along the long edge and clean finish both ends. I like to attach my sleeves after the quilt is bound. This way it can be easily removed should I ever decide it is not needed. I always form a tuck or folded pleat at the lower edge to allow for the circumference of the hanging rod or pole. This ensures that the quilt will hang flat and not have that bump you see in many quilts hanging at shows.

Quilt Label

Getting an embroidery machine was the best thing that ever happened to my quilt labels. In my early years I would just hand write a label with a fabric marker. Those labels were functional but not very pretty. Then I moved on to using my ink-jet printer, that worked well, but with multiple washings I find the labels fade. Now I prefer to embroider all my labels and I just use a standard format and switch out the fonts and the colors.

There are many options for quilt labels and I highly recommend labeling your quilts. I always include the name of the quilt, my name, my city, the date, and just recently I've been including the type of batting as that is helpful information to have for laundering.

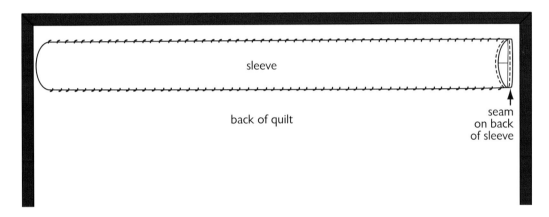

Fig. 8. Hanging sleeve

Fig. 10. Samples of quilt labels

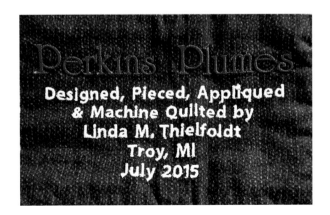

Midnight in Baltimore, 80" x 80"
Pieced and quilted by Linda Thielfoldt

MIDNIGHT IN BALTIMORE

· · · · · · · · · · · ·

Block Size: 18" x 18"

This quilt features nine different appliqué blocks along with a pieced border. The various black background fabrics lend a sense of drama to the quilt and the vibrant hues of the fabrics used in the motifs illuminate this quilt. The rickrack in between each block and around the borders adds a fun element.

Materials and Fabrics Needed

Black Prints – (9) 1 yard cuts for blocks and borders

Multi-Color Scraps – 2-3 yards in green, pink, gold, blue, and red

Lime Green Rickrack –

    17 yards of 1½" wide jumbo rickrack

    17 yards of ³⁄₁₆" wide large rickrack

Lime Green – ¾ yard for binding

Backing – 5 yards of 44" WOF your choice of fabric

Batting – Queen size quilt batt

Fusible Web – 12–13 yards of Wonder Under

Pencil – for marking fusible web

Glue stick – for applying the rickrack temporarily

Threads – for piecing, appliqué, and quilting

> *Note*
>
> I prefer to match the color of thread to the fabric when doing the buttonhole stitching so you may want to have lots of colors on hand.

Cutting

Black Prints

(9) 18½" x 18½" squares for center blocks

(12) 18½" x 8½" rectangles for border units

(4) 8½" x 8½" squares for border corners

Lime Green

(8) 2" x WOF strips for binding.

> ***Note***
> If you prefer a wider binding use the width measurement you prefer.

All other fabrics will be used for appliqué.

Piecing and Appliqué

Prepare the Appliqué

Begin by tracing around all appliqué shapes onto the paper side of the fusible web. Appliqué patterns are found on pp. 82–86. I use a mechanical pencil for this process and place the pieces together by color and also similar shapes. You don't need to leave much room between like pieces that will utilize the same fabric. For example, leaves that will be cut from the same fabric. This makes it easy to plan the fusing process and minimizes cutting of the fusible paper appliqué pieces before you apply them to the fabric. At this point you will have to decide on colors, use the photo of the quilt as your guide. It is often helpful to label similar looking pieces either with a number or a name.

Cut out all the fused appliqué pieces but do not remove the paper backing. It's a good idea at this point to count the shapes to make sure you have everything prepared and ready to go.

Appliqué the Blocks

Start by finding the center of each of the 18½" squares of fabric. I like to fold it on the diagonal corner to corner. Finger press so you can see the line. If the fold line is not visible enough I will often use chalk to draw a faint line corner to corner. Referring to the quilt photograph on p. 22 begin placing the cut out shapes onto the backing fabric. Make sure things that need to be tucked under are, and that the colors and placement are to your liking. Remember, it is not important that every piece be exactly placed. If there are multiple layers of a particular element, it may be helpful to pre-fuse them using the appliqué pressing sheet. I often do that with the flowers.

Once you have everything in place you need to remove the paper backing and start the fusing process. Follow the manufacturer's instructions for the fusible you have chosen to use. It is often helpful to score the backing paper with a pin to help peel the paper more easily. Continue the process until you have all 9 blocks completed. Use a buttonhole stitch

and matching thread stitch around all appliqué pieces in each block. Be sure to use a locking stitch at the beginning and ending of each stitching line.

Piecing the Blocks

Once you have decided on a layout it is a simple matter of sewing the blocks together. You are making a nine-patch so you will sew three (3) rows of three (3) blocks. Sew with a ¼" seam.

Add the Rickrack

I chose to sew the rickrack down by hand but you could also use your machine if you prefer. To begin, lay out pieces of rickrack on each of the block seams. If you happen to have a smaller piece or are trying to save yardage, you may have to piece the rickrack. Make sure all your joined pieces are hidden under a piece going the opposite direction. It is not necessary to actually piece the rickrack if it falls under another piece going the opposite way—you can just butt the rickrack together and glue baste it in place. Glue baste all the rickrack in place, centering it over the seams, then let it dry. Appliqué the rickrack to the quilt blocks using a matching thread (fig. 1).

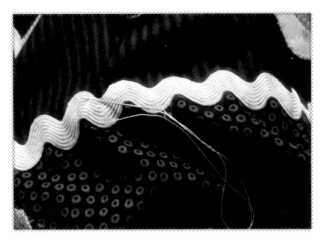

Fig. 1. Appliqué the rickrack to the seams of the quilt blocks

Designer Tip

Because you will be adding the rickrack I pressed the seams open to minimize bulk. I rarely do this because it makes for a weaker seam but in this case it made sense.

Borders

With right sides together, join three (3) border pieces per side. Attach the jumbo rickrack to the border strips making sure that you take into account the ¼" seam that is necessary to join the borders to the center of the quilt. I found it easier to trim off one edge of the jumbo rickrack before I added it to each border. It took a little time but the accuracy will be worth it. Take care with the position of the rickrack. You should be able to have the ends match up around the center of the quilt. Refer to the quilt photograph on p. 22 for placement. Glue baste, let dry, and then stitch in place.

Sew the top and bottom borders to the quilt center using a ¼" seam allowance. It's important to pin at frequent intervals. Press the seam, making sure that the rickrack seam is flat and not folded back on itself. Join the 8½" squares to the remaining two (2) side border units and press the seam open. Apply to the quilt.

Apply the remaining jumbo rickrack in the same manner to the perimeter of the quilt as instructed above, overlapping the rickrack at the corners. Machine stitch around the perimeter of the quilt for security and stability.

Completing the Quilt

If using 44" fabric, cut backing yardage into two (2) equal lengths 90" long x WOF, take time to trim selvages off the fabric before sewing the seam. Piece backing pieces together and sew along the trimmed edge using ¼" seam. Press seam to one side for security and strength. Layer the quilt top, batting and backing. Quilt the layers. MIDNIGHT IN BALTIMORE was longarm machine quilted using a variety of background stitches and some feathers in the borders. Appliqué pieces were quilted for emphasis and security.

Binding

For binding preparation and application refer to the General Quiltmaking Instructions, p. 20.

Don't forget to label your quilt!

> ### Note
> A 2" wide strip makes approximately ⁵⁄₁₆" wide finished binding. Adjust the size of the strip to your preferred size if you like.

Quilt assembly

On My Way to Baltimore, 42" x 54"
Pieced and quilted by Linda Thielfoldt

ON MY WAY TO BALTIMORE

Finished Block Size: 6"

This wall quilt is the one that started it all. A lovely basket of flowers and a sweet bird are the centerpiece of this charming quilt and are surrounded by twenty-four scrappy Log Cabin blocks. A small border and matching binding finish off the quilt.

Materials and Fabrics Needed

Tan Print – 1 yard for center of the quilt

Scraps – 1½–2 yards for Log Cabin blocks, lights and darks

Red Prints – (3) Fat quarters for appliqué (also can be used in logs)

Green Prints – (3) Fat quarters for appliqué (also can be used in logs)

Gold Scraps – 5" x 5" for appliqué

Red Print – 1 yard for outer border and binding

Backing – 2¾ yards of your choice of fabric

Batting – 48" x 58" piece of your choice

Fusible Web – 1 yard of Wonder Under

Threads – for piecing, appliqué, and quilting

Note

I prefer to match the color of thread to the fabric when doing the buttonhole stitching so you may want to have lots of colors on hand.

RIGHT: ON MY WAY TO BALTIMORE, detail, notice the scribble stitches around the appliqué

Cutting

Tan

(1) 24½" x 36½" rectangle to be used for the center background

Red

(5) 3½" x WOF strips for outer border

(5) 2" x WOF strips for binding

Note

If you prefer a wider binding use the width measurement you prefer.

Log Cabin Blocks

Finished Size 6"x6"

Begin by cutting your scraps into 1¼" wide strips. They may vary in length due to scraps, but that is perfectly okay as you will be cutting them into various smaller length pieces.

Sort the strips into piles of lights, mediums, and darks. You want all light on one side but can use some medium and dark fabrics on the opposite side as long as there is enough contrast between the two (2) sides

Fig. 1. Log Cabin block finished size 6" x 6"

I love mixing up lots of fabrics and you can use any color combination you like. In the quilt I used reds and greens as the medium/dark fabrics and all creams and tans for the light.

From each pile cut the following sizes:

1¼" x 1¼"	(32) light	(24) dark
1¼" x 2"	(32) light	(24) dark
1¼" x 2¾"	(32) light	(24) dark
1¼" x 3½"	(32) light	(24) dark
1¼" x 4¼"	(32) light	(24) dark
1¼" x 5"	(32) light	(24) dark
1¼" x 5¾"	(32) light	(24) dark
1¼" x 6½"	(32) light	(24) dark

Prepare the Appliqué

Trace all appliqué shapes onto the paper side of the fusible web using a mechanical pencil. Appliqué pattern is on p. 87. At this point you will have to decide on colors, use the photo of the quilt as your guide. Cut out all the fusible pieces using paper scissors or snips, utilize the Halo method described on p. 16.

Since the center of the quilt may be bigger than your ironing board it is helpful to start in the middle, lay out what fits on your ironing board, and then moving from left to right, fuse the other elements in place. If you have a large piece of corrugated cardboard you can lay the center fabric on that and then place all the elements to your liking. Once they are where you want them you can press just enough to hold them and then move the piece to your ironing board for a more complete pressing.

Once everything is fused in place it's time to do the buttonhole stitching. Choose a color to start with and complete all the stitching in that color. Switch to another and continue until all the pieces are stitched down. Remember to do a lock stitch at the start and end of each pass.

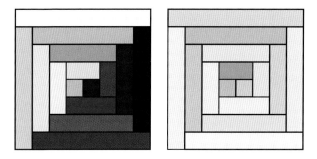

Fig. 2. Log Cabin block light and dark fabrics on the left and all light fabrics on right

Log Cabin Border

You Will Need to Make:

    (20) Log Cabin blocks that contain both light and dark fabrics as well as

    (4)   Log Cabin blocks made from all light fabrics.

    Follow piecing diagram (fig. 2). Press all seams away from the center square as you construct the blocks. Trim up each Log Cabin block to 6½" x 6½" square. Don't skip this step.

Following the quilt layout, sew four (4) Log Cabin blocks together for both the top and bottom borders. Pay close attention to orientation of the lights and darks, the dark edge of the Log Cabin blocks should be touching the center panel. Sew together using ¼" seam. Attach top and bottom borders to center of quilt, pinning carefully. Sew six (6) Log Cabin blocks together in the same manner as above, again pay attention to the orientation. Sew the four (4) light only Log Cabin blocks to each end of the two (2) remaining border strips. Sew the side borders to the quilt with the dark edge of the Log Cabin blocks touching the center panel. See quilt assembly, p. 32.

> ### Designer Tip
> Since there is so much going on in the Log Cabin blocks, I pressed the border toward the center (light) of the quilt, which is not normally what I would do. All those seams make for extra bulk I don't want to deal with so I broke one of the rules to always press to the dark. Be sure to trim up any loose thread so they don't show through.

Final Border

Measure the quilt on both long sides and cut two (2) strips of your border fabric to that length.

Pin to the quilt and sew with a ¼" seam. Press toward the border fabric away from the Log Cabin blocks. Repeat the process for the top and bottom borders.

Completing the Quilt

Cut the backing yardage into two (2) equal lengths 1½ yards each and trim selvages off the fabric before sewing the center seam. Piece backing pieces together, sewing along the trimmed edges using ¼" seam, backstitch at the beginning and ending of the seam. Press seam to one side for security and strength. Layer the quilt top, batting, and backing. Quilt the layers. ON MY WAY TO BALTIMORE was longarm machine quilted using a variety of feather motifs and a nice background fill. You may notice that around the appliqué and the feather motifs in the corners I have quilted some very small stitching. I call this scribble stippling and it is exactly what it sounds like. I like how it sets the motifs and the appliqué pieces apart and really lets them shine. If you want to give it a try just draw a line ½" around each motif and stitch within that line with a scribble stipple that is very small and dense. See the photo detail on p. 29. Once those are in place you can add in the background fill.

In the Log Cabin border I treated the color areas as triangles and placed triangular shaped feather motifs in each of those areas.

Binding

For binding preparation and application refer to the General Quiltmaking Instructions, p. 20.

Don't forget to label your quilt!

Quilt assembly

Pieced and quilted by Linda Thielfoldt. In this alternate version of ON MY WAY TO BALTIMORE, I simplified the quilt by adding two borders in place of the Log Cabin blocks. Inner border was cut 2½" and the outer border 6½" wide.

Chatham County, 51" x 51"
Pieced and quilted by Linda Thielfoldt

CHATHAM COUNTY

· · · · · · · · · · · ·

Block Size: 18"

This quilt is your typical nineteenth-century four-block quilt. Simplicity and style all rolled into one quilt. Made up of only three colors (burgundy, green, and cream), the toile border fabric adds a bit of panache. The alternate colorway, p. 38, showcases brown and pink fabrics and features a pieced background in each block. The brown and pink border fabric shows how effective a stripe print can be, thus making the quilt look more involved than it actually is.

Materials and Fabrics Needed

Cream Print – 1½ yards for background and border
   triangles (use a tone-on-tone print)
Green – (1) Fat quarter for center medallions
Dark Green – (1) Fat quarter for leaves
Burgundy Toile Print – ¾ yard for flower leaf
   Or (4) Fat quarters if you want them scrappy
Dark Burgundy Print – ¾ yard for inner triangle border
Burgundy Print – ½ yard for binding
Batting – 58" x 58" square of your choice
Backing – 3½ yards fabric of your choice
Fusible Web – 2 yards of Wonder Under
Pencil – for marking fusible web
Threads – for piecing, appliqué, and quilting

Cutting

Cream Tone-on-Tone

(4) 18½" x 18½" squares for center blocks

(6) 7¼" x 7¼" squares for inner border, cut each square on the diagonal twice to make twenty four (24) triangles for inner border

Dark Burgundy

(5) 7¼" x 7¼" squares, cut each square on the diagonal twice to make twenty (20) triangles for inner border side pieces

(2) 7¼" x 7¼" squares, cut each square on the diagonal once to make four (4) triangles for inner border corners

Burgundy Toile Print

(6) 6 ½" x WOF strips for outer border

Burgundy Binding

(7) 2" x WOF strips for binding

Note

If you prefer a wider binding use the width measurement you prefer.

All other fabrics will be used for appliqué.

Prepare the Appliqué

Trace all appliqué shapes onto the paper side of the fusible web using a mechanical pencil. Appliqué pattern is on p. 88. At this point you will have to decide on colors. Use the photo of the quilt as your guide. Cut out all the fusible pieces using paper scissors or snips, utilize the Halo method described on p.16. Leave the backing paper on until just before you are ready to fuse the pieces to the background squares.

Appliqué the Blocks

Start by finding the center of the 18½" squares. I like to fold it on the diagonal corner to corner. Finger press so you can see the line. Referring to the quilt photo begin placing the cut out shapes onto the backing fabric. Make sure things that need to be tucked under are, and that the colors and placement are to your liking. Remember, it is not important that every piece be exactly placed. Once you have everything in place you need to remove the paper backing and start the fusing process. Follow the manufacturer's instructions for the fusible you have chosen to use. It is often helpful to score the backing paper with a pin to help peel the paper more easily. Continue the process until you have all four (4) blocks completely fused. Using a buttonhole stitch and matching thread, stitch around all appliqué pieces in each block. Be sure to use a locking stitch at the beginning and ending of each stitching line.

Piecing the Blocks

Once you have decided on a layout it is a simple matter of sewing the blocks together. You are basically making a four-patch so you will sew two (2) rows of two (2) blocks. Sew with a ¼" seam and press each seam so they nest together.

Triangle Pieced Border

Following the color layout in the photo, stitch together border triangles. For the sides sew eleven (11) triangles together alternating colors and beginning and ending the border row with a cream triangle. Make four (4) pieced border units (fig. 1). Sew to the center of the quilt and press toward the middle blocks. Once all four (4) sides are on the quilt add the four (4) burgundy border triangles (fig. 2). The corner triangles are a bit bigger and once they are attached you will trim to the correct size.

Outer Border

Piece together the toile border strips. I often piece all of them together at one time and then just cut to the proper length and let the seams fall where they may. A busy print is the perfect choice to utilize that time-saving trick. If your border print is more obvious you may want to plan where your seam lines end up. Measure the top and bottom border edge and make a note of the length. Cut two (2) borders from your sewn strip to the measured length and pin each border to the center of the quilt. Sew with a ¼" seam and press toward the border. Measure the opposite two (2) sides of the quilt and make a note of the length. Cut two (2) border strips to those measurements and add to the quilt in the same manner. Press toward the border fabric. See quilt assembly, p. 38.

Completing the Quilt

If using 44" wide fabric, cut backing yardage into two (2) equal lengths, take time to

Fig. 1. Pieced border unit

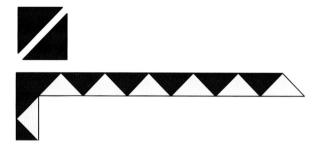

Fig. 2. Corner triangles

trim selvages off the fabric before sewing the seam. Piece backing pieces together and sew along the trimmed edge using a ¼" seam. Press the seam to one side for security and strength. Layer the quilt top, batting, and backing. Quilt the layers. CHATHAM COUNTY was longarm machine quilted using a crosshatch design in the center around the appliqué motifs extending into the cream triangle fabric. The burgundy triangles were quilted with a feather motif in contrasting thread. The toile border was quilted in a simple cable design.

Binding

For binding preparation and application refer to the General Quiltmaking Instructions, p. 20.

Don't forget to label your quilt!

> *Note*
>
> A 2" wide strip makes approximately 5/16" wide finished binding. Adjust the size of the strip to your preferred size if you like.

Quilt assembly

BELOW: CHATHAM COUNTY
51" x 51". Designed and quilted
by Linda Thielfoldt and pieced
by Janet Rose. This alternate
colorway shows a great use of
a stripe fabric in the border.
Additionally, the background
squares are pieced as well, giving
this quilt a really scrappy look.

Raspberry Limeade, 40" x 40"
Pieced and quilted by Linda Thielfoldt

RASPBERRY LIMEADE

· · · · · · · · · · · ·

Block size: 18"

This charming wallhanging combines one appliqué block along with some easy piecing for a delightful and quick project. Make it in some totally fun and updated fabrics and complete it in a weekend.

Materials and Fabrics Needed

Assorted pinks and lime greens along with a strong dark print (black) provide emphasis and contrast. This quilt also lends itself to a scrappy approach, just be sure to have good contrast with some light, medium, and dark fabrics.

Black – 1 yard for background and binding (tone-on-tone fabric)

Floral Print – ½ yard or (2) fat quarters for black triangles

Pink Polka Dot – ½ yard for inner border and appliqué

Light Lime Green – ¾ yard for corner triangles and appliqué stems

Scraps of pink and green – I used six (6) different pinks and three (3) different green fabrics for the flowers and leaves. Some of the fabrics were used in the pieced blocks.

Backing – 1½ yards of your choice of fabric

Binding – ¼ yard of black fabric

Batting – 48" x 48" square of your choice

Fusible Web – 1½ yards Wonder Under

Pieced blocks

Dark Pink Polka Dot – ½ yard

Light Pink Circle Print – ½ yard

Lime Green/Pink floral Print – ½ yard

Lime Green Polka Dot Print – ½ yard

Note

There will be enough fabric left over to use for some of the appliqué basket flowers and leaves.

Cutting

Black Tone-on-Tone

(1) 18" x 18" square

(4) 2" strips WOF to be used for binding

Dark Pink Polka Dot

(2) 2½" x 18" strips for inner border

(2) 2½" x 20½" strips for inner border

(4) 5⅞" squares, cut them in half diagonally to make eight (8) half-square triangles

Cut appliqué basket and flower pieces as desired – refer to the quilt photo.

Lime Green

(10) 5⅞" squares, cut them in half diagonally to make twenty (20) half square triangles

Cut appliqué leaves and stem pieces as desired – refer to the quilt photo.

Black/Pink/Lime Green Print

(10) 5⅞" squares, cut them in half diagonally to make twenty (20) half square triangles

Light Pink Circle Print

(32) 3" x 3" squares

Cut appliqué basket and flower pieces as desired – refer to the quilt photo.

Lime Green/Pink Floral Print

(32) 3" x 3" squares

Cut appliqué leaves and flower pieces as desired – refer to the quilt photo.

Light Lime Green

(2) 11" x 11" squares, cut in half diagonally to make four (4) half square triangles

> **Note**
>
> These are cut slightly oversize to allow for trimming after construction.

Piecing and Appliqué

Blocks

Build the 4-patch blocks and half-square blocks. Press all seams to the dark except for the middle 4-patch units, you will want to alternate the seam allowance on these. Press them so they lay nice and flat (figs. 1a–c).

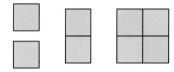

Fig 1a. Four-patch block

Fig 1b. Half-square block

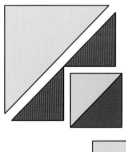 

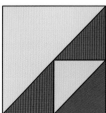

Fig 1c. Corner block, make 4

Appliqué

Trace all appliqué shapes onto the paper side of the fusible web using a mechanical pencil. Appliqué pattern is on p. 88. At this point you will have to decide on colors. Use the photo of the quilt as your guide. Cut out all the fusible pieces using paper scissors or snips, utilizing the Halo method described on p. 16. Leave the backing paper on until just before you are ready to fuse the pieces to the background squares.

Appliqué the Blocks

Start by finding the center of the 18½" square of fabric by folding it on the diagonal corner to corner. Finger press so you can see the line. If the fold line is not visible enough I will often use chalk to draw a faint line corner to corner. Referring to the quilt photo begin placing the cut out shapes onto the backing fabric. Make sure things that need to be tucked under are, and that the colors and placement are to your liking. Remember, it is not important that every piece be exactly placed. If there are multiple layers of a particular element, it may be helpful to pre-fuse them using the appliqué pressing sheet. I often do that with flowers. Once you have everything in place you need to remove the paper backing and start the fusing process. Follow the manufacturer's instructions for the fusible you have chosen to use. It is often helpful to score the backing paper with a pin to help peel the paper more easily. Using a buttonhole stitch and matching thread stitch around all appliqué pieces in each block. Be sure to use a locking stitch at the beginning and ending of each stitching line.

Complete all appliqué before assembling the rest of the quilt.

Quilt Top Assembly

Attach the pink inner border to the center appliqué square.

Referring to the quilt photo (p. 39) or assembly diagram, arrange the pieced units according to the layout guide. Be sure to check for proper placement before construction as turning a block the wrong way can throw off the whole layout. Press after each step.

Once you have attached the four outer corner triangles it may be necessary to trim them to square things up, the pattern dimensions allow for this.

Layer the top, batting, and backing. Quilt as desired.

Binding

For binding preparation and application refer to the General Quiltmaking Instructions, p. 20.

Don't forget to label your quilt!

Quilt assembly

RIGHT: RASPBERRY LIMEADE
40" x 40". Designed and quilted by Linda Thielfoldt and pieced by Janet Rose. Rich saturated colors give this alternate version a primitive look.

Maryland Rose, 53" x 53"
Pieced and quilted by Linda Thielfoldt

On My Way to BALTIMORE ❧ *Linda Thielfoldt*

MARYLAND ROSE

· · · · · · · · · · · ·

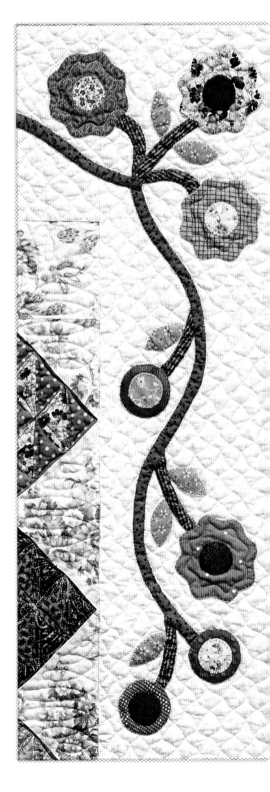

Block Size: 18" x 18"

This charming quilt was made with some lovely floral fabrics and just whispers pure romance. The single central block is surrounded by four different borders. The first border is made up of twelve pieced triangle blocks and the second features an appliqué floral vine in just two of the corners, leaving room for some fabulous quilting. The third border consists of triangles pieced from two fabrics and the final outer border is a tone-on-tone fabric that allows your quilting to really shine.

Materials and Fabrics Needed

Cream – 1¾ yards for center block background and appliqué border

Burgundy – 1 yard for outer border (tone-on-tone fabric)

Medium Scale Floral – 1¼ yard for triangles in border 1 and 3

Green – ¾ yard for triangles in border 3

Green – 1 yard for binding – note binding was cut on bias

> **Note**
> If using straight cut binding you need ½ yard of fabric

Pieced Triangles and Appliqué:

Fat quarters

10–12 different pink/burgundy prints

10–12 different green prints

½ yard dark green for appliqué vine

Backing – 4¼ yards your choice of fabric

Batting – 60" x 60" square of your choice

Fusible Web – 3 yards

Cutting

Cream

(1) 18½" x 18½" square for center block background

(4) 6½" x WOF strips, these will be used for the appliqué border background

Medium Scale Floral

 (8) 7¼" x 7¼" squares, then cut twice on the diagonal (these will be used on the sides of both the first border and the 3rd border)

 (4) 3⅞" x 3⅞" squares, then cut once on the diagonal (these will be used toward the corners of the first border)

(4) 3½" x 3½" squares (these will be used in the very corner of the first border)

Green Check

 (7) 7¼" x 7¼" squares, cut twice on the diagonal to yield twenty-eight (28) triangles (these will be used on the 3rd border)

Pieced Blocks for First Border

You will be making twelve (12) triangle blocks pieced from nine (9) smaller triangles (fig. 1).

Fig. 1.

For each triangle block from assorted fat quarters cut the following

 Dark: (2) 3¼" x 3¼" squares, cut twice on the diagonal

 Light: (1) 3¼" x 3¼" squares, cut twice on the diagonal

Final Border
Burgundy Tone-on-Tone

(6) 6¼" x WOF strips

Binding
Green Check

Enough 2" strips to make 230" of binding.

Note

If you're using straight cut binding you will need seven (7) strips.

Appliqué

Trace all appliqué shapes onto the paper side of the fusible web using a mechanical pencil. Appliqué pattern is on p. 89. At this point you will have to decide on colors, use the photo of the quilt as your guide. Cut out all the fusible pieces using paper scissors or snips, utilize the Halo method described on p. 16. Leave the backing paper on until just before you are ready to fuse the pieces to the background squares.

Appliqué the Center Block

Start by finding the center of the cream square. Referring to the quilt photo begin placing the cut out shapes onto the backing fabric. Make sure things that need to be tucked under are, and that the colors and placement are to your liking. Remember, it is not important that every piece be exactly placed. Once you have everything in place remove the paper backing and start the fusing process. Follow the manufacturer's instructions for the fusible you have chosen to use. It is often helpful to score the backing paper with a pin to help peel the paper more easily. Using a buttonhole stitch and matching thread stitch around all appliqué pieces in each block. Be sure to use a locking stitch at the beginning and ending of each stitching line.

First Border Triangle Units

You will need to piece twelve (12) triangle units. For each triangle block you will need six (6) dark triangles and three (3) light triangles that you cut from the fat quarters.

Take one (1) dark and one (1) light triangle and sew together on the long edge. Make three (3) of these HST. Press seam to the dark. Lay them out as shown in fig. 1 (p. 46) and add the remaining dark triangles along the bottom edge. Piece in three (3) rows and then sew the rows together to complete the block. Press seam to one side.

Repeat this process for all twelve (12) triangle blocks. Mix up the fabrics and make them as scrappy or as coordinated as you like.

Layout the triangle units around the center square in a pleasing arrangement.

Each side will utilize three (3) triangle blocks.

This border piecing will utilize the triangle blocks, two (2) different size triangles, and the squares you cut from the medium floral fabric.

For the first two (2) sides, start and end each border set with a small floral triangle, three (3) pieced triangle blocks, and two (2) larger floral triangles in the middle. Piece as

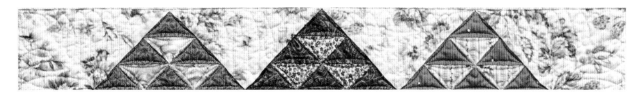

Fig. 2. One side of the first border made with pieced triangle blocks and two different size triangles cut from the medium floral fabric

shown in fig. 2 (p. 47) sew to center square and then press toward the center appliqué block.

For the remaining two (2) sides you will again start and end each border set with a small floral triangle, (3) pieced triangle blocks and (2) larger floral triangles in the middle. Piece as shown in fig. 2 (p. 47) and then add one of the medium floral squares to each end.

Sew to the center of the quilt and then press the seam toward the center appliqué block.

Appliqué Border (two)

The vine and floral design will be applied to the cream border fabric after it has been sewn to the center of the quilt.

Begin by measuring the center of your quilt. Cut two (2) of the four (4) strips you cut from the cream fabric to this measurement. Pin to the quilt and sew two (2) strips onto opposite sides. Press toward the cream. Again measure the quilt including the two (2) border strips you just added and cut the two (2) remaining border strips to that measurement. Sew the two (2) remaining strips onto the final two (2) edges of the quilt and press those two (2) seams toward the light border to minimize bulk at the triangle block edges.

Trace all appliqué shapes onto the paper side of the fusible web using a mechanical pencil. At this point you will have to decide on colors. Use the photo of the quilt as your guide. Cut out all the fusible pieces using paper scissors or snips, utilizing the Halo

method described on p. 16 for the larger pieces and fuse your chosen fabrics. Leave the backing paper on until just before you are ready to fuse the pieces to the background squares.

Referring to the quilt photo begin placing the cut out shapes onto the backing fabric in two (2) opposite corners. I find it helpful to place the vines first and then add the leaves and shorter stems to that. Lastly I add the flowers. Make sure things that need to be tucked under are, and that the colors and placement are to your liking. Remember, it is not important that every piece be exactly placed. Follow the manufacturer's instructions for the fusible you have chosen to use. It is often helpful to score the backing paper with a pin to help peel the paper more easily. Using a buttonhole stitch and matching thread, stitch around all appliqué pieces in each block. Be sure to use a locking stitch at the beginning and ending of each stitching line.

Pieced Border (three)

The border is made up of triangles cut from the medium floral print and the green check print (fig. 3). You will add six (6) floral and five (5) green triangles to each side. In order to avoid a miter of each corner, sew the borders on the quilt leaving off the green

Fig. 3. Detail of pieced border three

corner triangles. Then sew two (2) green triangles together, making four (4) sets, to form a triangle corner unit and proceed to sew to each of the four corners (fig. 3).

Final Border (four)

Piece together the border strips along the short ends. I often piece the border strips together end to end at one time and then just cut to length and let the seams fall where they may. The burgundy tone-on-tone print in this quilt makes that method a good one since the seams are barely visible. Busy or large prints may not work well with this method and you may want to plan how those kinds of fabrics match up when used in a wide border.

To apply the borders, measure the top and bottom border edge and make a note of the length(s), don't worry if they are slightly different. Cut two (2) borders from your sewn border strip and pin each border to the top and bottom edges of the quilt. Pinning is an important step if you want your border to come out correctly and not have a ripple. Sew with a ¼" seam and press toward the border. Measure the opposite two (2) sides of the quilt and make a note of the length(s). Cut two (2) border strips to those measurements and add to the quilt in the same manner. Press toward the border fabric (fig. 4).

Completing the Quilt

Cut backing yardage into two (2) equal lengths, take time to trim selvages off the fabric before sewing the center seam. Piece backing sections together along the trimmed

edge using a ¼" seam. Press seam to one side for security and strength. I like to leave the remaining selvages on the backing fabric for stability when loading and quilting the quilt. Layer the quilt top, batting, and backing and quilt as you wish. I used some floral designs in the open areas of the cream border along with relaxed crosshatching and a nice, dense background fill in for the center block sets off the appliqué nicely. The outer border features the same floral design as in the cream border but quilted with contrasting thread.

Binding

For binding preparation and application refer to the General Quiltmaking Instructions, p. 20.

Don't forget to label your quilt!

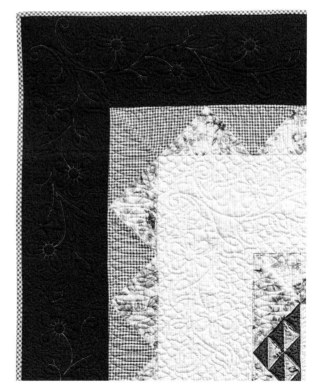

Fig. 4. Detail of borders with final border (four) added

Quilt assembly

LEFT: MARYLAND ROSE, 53" x 53". Designed and quilted by Linda Thielfoldt and pieced by Karen Lieberman. This alternate version shows how using a striking border print really adds drama. The small pieced triangles that surround the center block were swapped out for large triangles which simplified the process.

Tulip Splendor, 55" x 55"
Pieced and quilted by Linda Thielfoldt

TULIP SPLENDOR

· · · · · · · · · · · ·

Block Size: 20" x 20"

This fun and funky quilt proves that more color is better and the floral print fabric provides the color palette. Fun tulips and beautiful birds bring it all together and just shout *Spring!*

Materials and Fabrics Needed:

White Polka Dot – 2½ yards for center block, large triangles and outer border

Turquoise Polka Dot – 1 yard for border, flowers and binding

Assorted scraps or fat quarters – in greens, pinks, oranges, blues, turquoise, yellows for flowers and birds – this is where more is better.

Green – ½ yard for flower stems

> ### Note
> All the stems are cut from the same fabric. If you want to make them scrappy by all means do, just adjust your fabrics accordingly.

Green – (1) fat quarter for leaves

Lime Turquoise – (1) fat quarter for flower pot

Backing – 4 yards fabric

Batting – 60" x 60" square of your choice

Fusible Web – 3 yards

Thread – for appliqué and piecing

Cutting

White Polka Dot

- (4) 8" x WOF strips to be used for outer appliqué border
- (1) 20½" x 20½" square for center appliqué block
- (2) 16¾" x 16¾" squares to be used for appliqué triangles, do not cut into triangles just yet.

Turquoise Polka Dot

- (5) 2½" x WOF strips for border
- (6) 2" x WOF strips to be used for binding

Turquoise Floral Print

- (2) 15½" x 15½" squares, then cut once on the diagonal to be used for large triangles
- (4) 8" x 8" squares to be used for border corners

Appliqué

Trace all appliqué shapes onto the paper side of the fusible web using a mechanical pencil. Appliqué pattern is on p. 90. At this point you will have to decide on colors. Use the photo of the quilt as your guide. Cut out all the fusible pieces using paper scissors or snips. Fuse to fabric and then cut out.

Appliqué the Center Block

Start by finding the center of the white square. Referring to the quilt photo begin placing the cut out shapes onto the backing fabric. Make sure things that need to be tucked under are, and that the colors and placement

are to your liking. Once you have everything in place remove the paper backing and start the fusing process. Follow the manufacturer's instructions for the fusible you have chosen to use. It is often helpful to score the backing paper with a pin to help peel the paper more easily. Using a buttonhole stitch and matching thread stitch around all appliqué pieces in each block. Be sure to use a locking stitch at the beginning and ending of each stitching line (fig. 1).

Quilt Assembly

Floral Print Triangles

Sew two (2) triangles to opposite sides of the center block using a ¼" seam. Press toward the floral print. Sew the remaining two (2) triangles to the remaining sides and again press the seam toward the floral print (fig. 2, p. 54).

Fig. 1. Center block

Fig. 2. Floral print triangles sewn to the center block

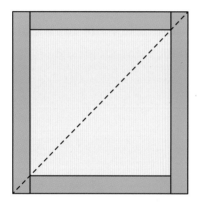

Fig. 3. Appliqué triangles and turquoise border cut on diagonal

> ## Designer Tip
>
> If your turquoise border extends more than ¼" beyond the floral print triangles you can square up and trim the quilt at this point. The outer border is cut to fit so if you need or want to square up the quilt at this point everything will still fit together nicely.

At this time you will need to trim the center of the quilt to 29" x 29" square. I often do this when using large triangles since it can be difficult to get the quilt to come out square and dealing with such large pieces cut on the bias can present issues as the quilt grows. I just lay my 6" x 24" ruler along the edge, lining up the 45° line on the edge of the triangle, while keeping the ¼" line exactly on the triangle point, and trim.

Appliqué Triangles and Turquoise Border

This step is a bit unorthodox but yields great results and makes the set in border super easy. Start with the 16¾" x 16¾" white polka dot squares and the 2½" x WOF turquoise border strips.

Cut four (4) strips 16¾" x 2½" long, sew to two (2) opposite sides of both squares. Press to the turquoise fabric. Cut four (4) strips 19¼" long, sew to the remaining two (2) sides of both squares, and press to the turquoise fabric. This will give you a square bordered on all sides. Next you will cut both bordered squares in half once on the diagonal this will give you the four (4) triangles you need to add to the center of the quilt (fig. 3).

Before you add to the center of the quilt you will want to appliqué the tulip motif on each triangle. It's much easier to deal with the smaller piece than the whole quilt. Follow appliqué instructions above.

Appliqué Border

Measure your quilt top on all sides. My version measured 40¼" on each side. Your measurement may vary from that dimension and that is perfectly OK. No matter what your measurement turns out to be, that is the length you will cut the borders strips. Do not attach to the quilt until after the appliqué is complete.

Cut four (4) of the white polka dot strips. The design used in the triangles is the same one used in the border. You need three (3) per side. Place the appliqué designs on these four border strips and appliqué following instruction above (fig, 4).

Add two (2) of the corner blocks to two (2) of the borders and press to the floral print. Sew the remaining two (2) borders onto the quilt using a ¼" seam and press to the turquoise border. Next take the remaining border with the corner blocks attached and pin to the quilt on the remaining two (2) sides. Take care to match up the seams at the corner block/border intersections since a misplaced seam line will really show. I like to pin on both sides of the seam allowance. If you pressed them correctly, they should nest together nicely. Sew the final borders on the quilt using a ¼" seam. Press.

Fig. 4. Detail of appliquéd border

Completing the Quilt

Cut backing yardage into two equal lengths, take time to trim selvages off the fabric before sewing the center seam. Piece backing sections together along the trimmed edge using a ¼" seam. Press seam to one side for security and strength. I like to leave the remaining selvages on the backing fabric for stability when loading and quilting the quilt. Layer the quilt top, batting, and backing and quilt as you wish.

Binding

For binding preparation and application refer to the General Quiltmaking Instructions, p. 20.

Don't forget to label your quilt!

Quilt assembly

LEFT: In this alternate version of TULIP SPLENDOR Linda opted to simplify the design by eliminating the triangle and border appliqué and instead used a lively floral print. The plain triangles are the perfect place for some fancy feather quilting.

Perkins Purple Plumes, 75" x 75"
Pieced and quilted by Linda Thielfoldt

PERKINS PURPLE PLUMES

Block Size: 18" x 18"

At the International Exhibition of 1862 held in London, Queen Victoria wore a gown of silk dyed with aniline purple, a synthetic dye better known as Mauveine. Mauveine had become the height of fashion after its accidental discovery in 1857 by chemistry student William Henry Perkin. While trying to develop a drug to fight malaria, Perkin was experimenting with a compound into which he dipped a piece of silk. The silk turned a reddish-purple color that would not wash out. He went on to set up a factory to produce the synthetic dye. All the fabrics in this quilt are reproduction and in various shades of "Perkins Purple" and present a different spin on the traditional two-color quilt. The simple plume motif is carried out in the appliqué, the quilting, and the border and the cream background ensures that your quilting will really show.

Materials and Fabrics Needed:

Cream Muslin – 6 yards for blocks, geese, and border
Purple Print – 1 yard for flying geese blocks
    1 fat quarter for corner squares (or scraps from appliqué)
    9 fat quarters for appliqué plumes
Binding – ¾ yard dark purple print
Backing – 5 yards 44" wide muslin or
    2½ yards 90" wide backing
Batting – Queen size quilt batt
Fusible Web – 2 yards
Thread – for appliqué and piecing

Cutting

Cream Muslin

> (9) 18½" x 18½" squares for appliqué blocks
>
> (108) 2⅞" x 2⅞" squares for flying geese backgrounds
>
> (8) 6½" x WOF strips for outer border

Purple Print

> (27) 5¼" x 5¼" squares for flying geese blocks

Purple Fat Quarters

> (4) 4½" x 4½" squares for the geese border corners. These can be all the same fabrics or all different.

Dark Purple Print

> (8) 2" x WOF strips for binding

Prepare the Appliqué

Trace the appliqué shapes onto the paper side of the fusible web using a mechanical pencil. Appliqué pattern is on p. 91. For each of the nine (9) blocks you will need four (4) plumes of the same fabric. Cut out all the fusible pieces using paper scissors or snips. Fuse to fabric and cut out. Since the shapes are detailed and not very big I don't utilize the Halo method described on p. 16.

Fig. 1. Zach helping with the buttonhole stitching

Appliqué the Center Blocks

Start by finding the center of the cream square. Referring to the quilt photo (p. 57) begin placing the plumes onto the backing fabric. Since the muslin is easy to see through I will do the first square and then lay the next one on top for placement. You can see the plumes through the fabric and it makes it super easy to get all the blocks placed the same way. Follow the manufacturer's instructions for the fusible you have chosen to use. It is often helpful to score the backing paper with a pin to help peel the paper more easily. Using a buttonhole stitch and matching thread stitch around all appliqué pieces in each block. Be sure to use a locking stitch at the beginning and ending of each stitching line.

It is very helpful when doing the buttonhole stitching to have some help. Zach is a great supervisor (fig. 1). He was part of every block and all the geese in this quilt.

Once you have the appliqué done on the plume blocks you can piece them together. Basically you are making a huge 9-patch. Alternate seams when pressing.

Flying Geese Border

Lots of geese! One hundred-eight (108) to be exact. Fear not though since you will be making four (4) at a time.

Start with one (1) of the 5¼" x 5¼" purple squares and four (4) of the 2⅞" x 2⅞" cream squares (fig. 2A).

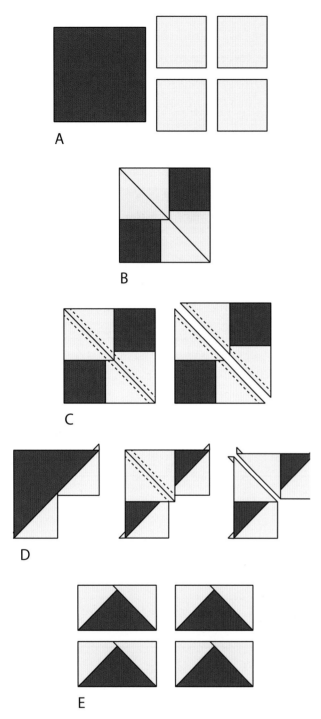

Fig. 2. Flying Geese for border

Place two (2) of the cream squares on top of the purple square with right sides together. They will go in opposite corners and overlap slightly. Be sure that the outer edges are aligned exactly. Draw a line across the center of the cream squares as shown (fig. 2B).

Sew on both sides of the line using a ¼" seam allowance. Cut on the line (fig. 2C).

Take the remaining two (2) cream squares and place on the corner of each of the two (2) units you just made as shown here. Again draw a line from corner to corner, sew on either side of the mark and then cut on the marked line. Press away from the purple triangle so that the block units lie flat and are easier to sew together (fig. 2D).

After pressing you will have four (4) geese units. Repeat the process until you have made one hundred-eight (108) geese (fig. 2D).

Sew twenty-seven (27) geese units together to make four (4) border strips. Press seams toward the purple triangle to allow for the geese to lay as flat as possible.

Borders

Attach two (2) of the geese border strips to two (2) opposite edges of the quilt. I find lots of pins are necessary. When stitching, be sure the quilt top is on the bottom and that the geese units are visible so that you can see the points of the triangles while sewing. You will be less likely to cut off any of the points as you sew if you can see them. Press seam away from the geese. For the remaining two (2) border strips, attach one (1) of the 4½" x 4½" purple squares to each end. Press to the squares. Pin the final two (2) borders to the quilt and again keeping the quilt on the bottom, sew ¼" seam along the edge. Press toward the center of the quilt.

Outer Border

Piece together the border strips along the short ends. Be sure to cut off the selvage ends before you piece them together. I usually piece the border strips together end to end at one time and then just cut to length and let the seams fall where they may. The cream muslin used in this quilt makes that method a good one since the seams are barely visible once quilted.

To apply the borders, measure the top and bottom border edge and make a note of the length(s). Don't worry if they are slightly different. Cut two (2) borders from the muslin sewn border strip using your measurements. Pin each border to the top and bottom edges of the quilt. Pinning is an important step if you want your border to come out correctly and not have a ripple. Sew with a ¼" seam and press toward the border away from the geese border. Measure the remaining two (2) sides of the quilt and make a note of the length(s). Cut two (2) border strips to those measurements and add to the quilt in the same manner. Press toward the border and away from the geese. See borders detail (fig. 3) and quilt assembly (p. 62).

Completing the Quilt

Cut backing yardage into two (2) equal lengths, take time to trim selvages off the fabric before sewing the center seam. Piece backing sections together along the trimmed edge using a ¼" seam. Press seam to one side for security and strength. I like to leave the remaining selvages on the backing fabric for stability when loading and quilting the quilt. Layer the quilt top, batting, and backing and quilt as you wish.

Binding

For binding preparation and application refer to the General Quiltmaking Instructions, p. 20.

Don't forget to label your quilt!

Fig. 3. Borders detail

Quilt assembly

LEFT: PERKINS PLUMES alternate features a lively border print and a red tone-on-tone print in place of the muslin. A lively all-over feather quilting design was a unique but effective choice for this quilt and is quilted right over the appliqué motifs.

Nottingham Pomegranate, 58" × 58"
Pieced and quilted by Linda Thielfoldt

NOTTINGHAM POMEGRANATE

· · · · · · · · · · · ·

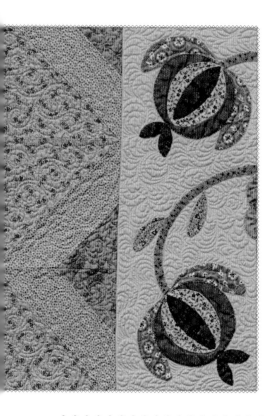

Note

If you want to match the print in the border to hide the seams you may need to purchase more fabric depending on the scale and repeat of your print.

Note

Binding strips were cut on the bias.

Block Size: 18" x 18"

The lively cheddar, pink, and fuchsia border fabric was what started it all.

Take a traditional antique block motif such as the pomegranate and mix it up with a fun and funky color combination and you take a vintage inspired quilt to a new level.

For a more traditional look to this quilt check out another color option on p. 69.

Materials and Fabrics Needed:

Solid Cheddar – 1½ yards for appliqué background blocks

Floral Print – 1½ yard for outer border (large scale print)

Medium Pink – 1 yard for paper-pieced border blocks

Cheddar Print – 1 yard for paper-pieced border blocks

Dark Pink Paisley Print – ½ yard for paper-pieced border blocks and center flower

Cheddar Prints – (4) fat quarters for leaves and flower parts

Dark Cheddar Print – ½ yard for vines

Dark Rose/ fuchsia Prints – (2) fat quarters for pomegranate parts

Stripe Fabric – ¾ yard for binding

Backing – 4 yards 44" wide fabric

Fusible Web – 3 yards

Batting – 60" x 60" piece

Thread – for appliqué and piecing

Newsprint Paper – 28 sheets for paper-pieced border blocks

Cutting

Cheddar Solid

(4) 18½" x 18½" squares for center appliqué blocks

Medium Pink Floral

(14) 7½" x 7½" squares to be used for paper-pieced border—cut once on the diagonal to yield twenty-eight (28) triangles

Cheddar Print

(28) 3½" x 10" rectangles to be used for paper-pieced border

Dark Pink Paisley Print

(14) 4¾" x 4¾" squares to be used for paper-pieced border—cut once on the diagonal to yield twenty-eight (28) triangles

Larger Cheddar Fuchsia Floral Print

(6) 8" x WOF strips to be used for outer border

Appliqué

Trace all appliqué shapes onto the paper side of the fusible web using a mechanical pencil. Appliqué pattern is on p. 92. At this point you will have to decide on colors. Use the photo of the quilt as your guide. Cut out all the fusible pieces using paper scissors or snips, utilizing the Halo method described on p. 16 unless the pieces are small.

Appliqué the Center Block

Start by finding the center of the cheddar squares. Referring to the quilt photo begin placing the cut out shapes onto the cheddar background fabric. Make sure things that need to be tucked under are, and that the colors and placement are to your liking. Remember, it is not important that every piece be exactly placed. Follow the manufacturer's instructions for the fusible you have chosen to use. It is often helpful to score the backing paper with a pin to help peel the paper more easily. Using a buttonhole stitch and matching thread, stitch around all appliqué pieces in each block. Be sure to use a locking stitch at the beginning and ending of each stitching line.

Border Blocks Assembly

Paper Pieced Blocks

One of my favorite methods of piecing odd shaped or complicated blocks is using paper piecing (figs. 2 and 3, p. 66). It's accurate and pretty simple if you pre-cut your shapes to the proper size. To start put in a slightly larger needle (90) and put your stitch length on 1.5.

In order to have the seams pressed the correct way for ease of "nesting" you need to start half the blocks with the larger triangle and half the blocks with the smaller. This will

Fig. 1. Appliquéd center block

Fig. 2. Paper-pieced border block, pattern below

ensure that the seams are going in the proper direction upon completion and will make putting the border blocks together an easy task. Start with the outer triangle, add the cheddar strip in the middle and sew ¼" seam. Press and trim seam allowance, and add the final triangle. Repeat for remaining fourteen (14) blocks making sure to start the process with the opposite triangle and chain piecing them for quick results. If you piece the border blocks in this manner then they will nest together nicely when you alternate them for piecing the border.

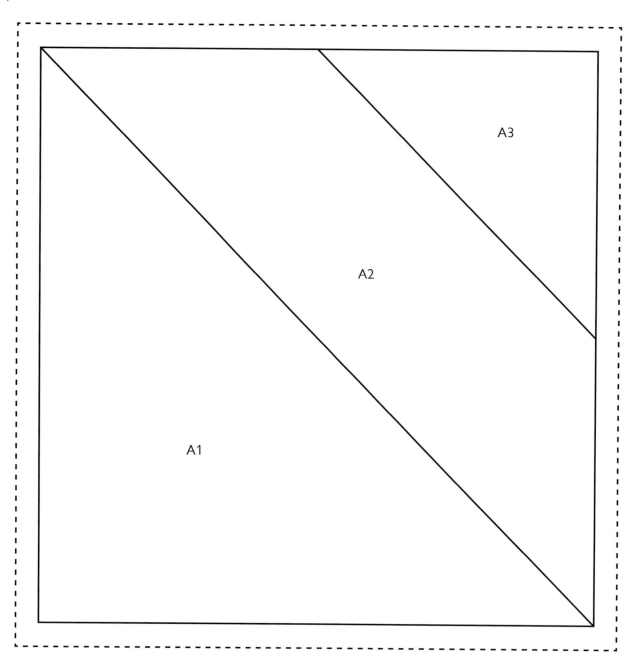

Fig. 3. Border block paper-piecing pattern, shown at 100%

Once you have the blocks complete and pressed, it is time to trim them down. On the paper pieced pattern there is a ¼" seam allowance on all edges. Trim all twenty-eight (28) blocks on that line. At this point you can remove the paper from the back taking care not to stretch the blocks too much as there is a lot of bias. I like to use sizing on every block before I remove the paper.

It is now easy to just sew the blocks together and you will quickly see how that alternating the starting triangle comes in handy. Pay attention when you layout all the blocks making sure to alternate them every other one so when you go to join them the seam lines of the paper piecing will nest nicely. If you forgot you can always press the seams back the other way. The design is obvious, so perfectly matching the seams is important. Pinning and pressing correctly are two important aspects of this border.

Border Block Layout

You will sew six (6) blocks together for two (2) borders and eight (8) together for the other two (2). Pay close attention to the design as it is easy to get them mixed up and going the wrong way. See quilt assembly diagram.

Once you have the block borders sewn into strips, attach the two (2) border strips made up of six (6) blocks to two (2) opposite edges of the quilt. I find lots of pins helpful. When stitching, be sure the quilt top is on the bottom and that the pieced triangle units are visible so that you can see the points of the triangle intersections while sewing. You will be less likely to cut off any of the points as you sew if you can see them. Press seam toward the center of the quilt. Pin the remaining two (2) border strips to the quilt center and follow the same procedure when you sew the seam. Press seam to the center of the quilt.

Outer Border

Piece together the border strips along the short ends. Be sure to cut off the selvage ends before you piece them together. I usually piece the border strips together end to end at one time and then just cut to length, letting the seams fall where they may. The busy floral print used in this quilt makes that method a good one since the seams are barely visible once quilted but if you want to take the time to match the print it is easy enough to do, you just need more fabric. For this quilt I would allow eight (8) strips WOF if you want to match the print.

To apply the borders measure the top and bottom border edge and make a note of the length(s). Don't worry if they are slightly different. Cut two (2) borders from the floral border strip using your measurements. Pin each border to the top and bottom edges of the quilt. Pinning is an important step if you want your border to come out correctly and not have a ripple. Sew with a ¼" seam and press toward the border away from the pieced border. Measure the remaining two (2) sides of the quilt and make a note of the length(s). Cut two (2) border strips to those measurements and add to the quilt in the same manner. Press toward the border and away from the pieced border. See quilt assembly diagram (p. 68).

Completing the Quilt

Cut backing yardage into two (2) equal lengths. Take time to trim selvages off the fabric before sewing the center seam. Piece backing sections together along the trimmed edge using a ¼" seam. Press seam to one side for security and strength. I like to leave the remaining selvages on the backing fabric for stability when loading and quilting the quilt. Layer the quilt top, batting, and backing and quilt as you wish.

Binding

For binding preparation and application refer to the General Quiltmaking Instructions, p. 20.

Don't forget to label your quilt!

Fig. 4. Detail of binding on scalloped edge

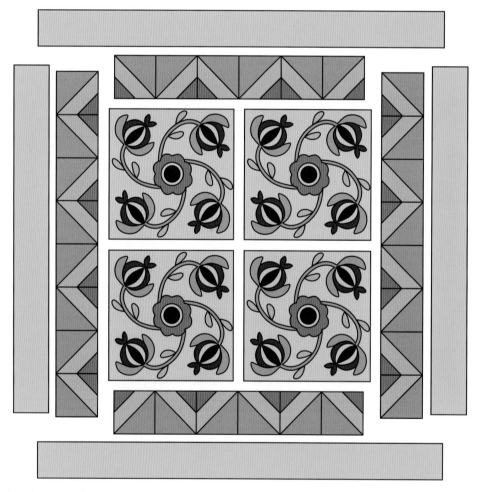

Quilt assembly

Red, green, and cream fabrics give this alternate colorway of
NOTTINGHAM POMEGRANATE a real traditional look. The large floral border
print ties in nicely with the center appliqué blocks.

Seville, 56" x 56"
Pieced and quilted by Linda Thielfoldt

SEVILLE
· · · · · · · · · · · ·

Block Size: 13½" x 13½"

Simple chain blocks that extend into the border provide the backdrop for this traditional appliqué block that features reproduction fabrics. The wide border gives you a wonderful opportunity to showcase some special quilting.

Materials and Fabrics Needed:

Dark Green Check – ⅓ yard for the large green appliqué leaves

Medium Green Print – (1) fat quarter for appliqué leaves

Dark Purple Print – (1) fat quarter for center appliqué medallion

Purple/Green Stripe – (1) fat quarter for center appliqué medallion

Dark Green/Purple Paisley – ¾ yard for plumes appliqué

Dark Pink Print – (1) fat quarter for appliqué berries

Light Green Swirl Print – 2½ yards used for block background and chain blocks

Dark Purple Print – ¾ yard for chain blocks

Dark Green Polka Dot – 2 yards for border

Light Green – ⅝ yard for binding

Batting – 63" x 63" piece

Backing – 3¾ yards

Fusible Web – 2¼ yards

Thread – for appliqué and piecing

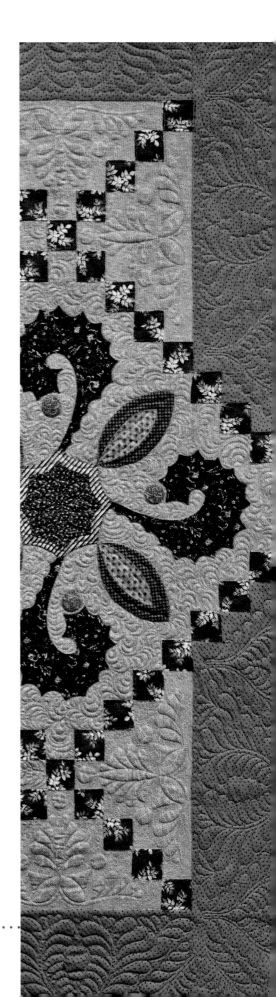

Quilt Components

You will be making two (2) different chain blocks that form the background for the appliqué and extend into the border. You need five (5) full chain blocks (fig. 1) and four (4) partial chain blocks (fig. 2) in addition to four (4) plain squares of background fabric. The appliqué motifs are added after the quilt top is assembled.

Cutting

Full Chain Block (Make 5)

Purple Paisley Print

(85) 2" x 2" squares (A)

Light Green Swirl Print

(20) 2" x 2" squares (C)

(20) 2" x 5" rectangles (B)

(20) 2" x 8" rectangles (D)

(20) 2" x 11" rectangles (E)

For the Plain Squares

Light Green Swirly Print

(4) 14" x 14" squares

For the Partial Chain Blocks (Make 4)

Light Green Swirl Print

(4) 2" x 2" squares (C)

(4) 5" x 2" rectangles (B)

(4) 8" x 2" rectangles (D)

(4) 11" x 2" rectangles (E)

Dark Green Polka Dot Print

(8) 2" x 2" squares (F)

(8) 3½" x 2" rectangles (G)

(8) 5" x 2" rectangles (H)

(8) 6½" x 2" rectangles (I)

Purple Paisley Print:

(36) 2" x 2" squares (A)

For the Borders

Dark Green Polka Dot Print:

(4) 8" x 14" rectangles

(4) 8" x 21½" rectangles

Block Assembly

Chain blocks

Construct the center 9-patch first for each of the five (5) chain blocks. Add the purple squares and light green rectangles as shown in the piecing diagram (fig. 3, p 78).

Partial Chain Blocks

The partial chain block is constructed in the same manner with the exception of the fabrics. The dark green fabrics will appear on

Fig. 1. Full Chain Block

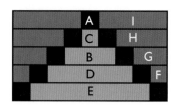

Fig. 2. Partial Chain Block

On My Way to BALTIMORE 🙚 *Linda Thielfoldt*

the outer edges of the block and the light green on the interior (fig. 4).

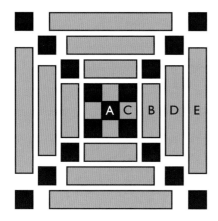

Fig. 3. Full Chain Block piecing

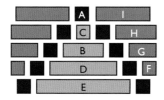

Fig. 4. Partial Chain Block piecing

Quilt Assembly

The complete quilt top is constructed before adding the appliqué. Follow the quilt assembly diagram (p. 74). The center of the quilt is pieced just like a giant 9-patch from the chain blocks and plain fabric squares.

For the top and bottom borders sew two (2) of the partial chain blocks to the 8" x 14" rectangles. Sew to the quilt center. Press toward the border.

For the side borders, sew the remaining two (2) partial chain blocks to the 8" x 21½" rectangles. Sew to the quilt center. Press toward the border.

Appliqué

Trace all appliqué shapes onto the paper side of the fusible web using a mechanical pencil. Appliqué pattern is on p. 92. At this point you will have to decide on colors. Use the photo of the quilt as your guide. Cut out all the fusible pieces using paper scissors or snips, utilizing the Halo method described on p. 16, unless the pieces are small. Fuse to fabric and cut out on drawn lines.

Appliqué the Blocks

This quilt is a bit different in that you appliqué the "blocks" after the quilt is pieced. Start by finding the center of each pieced square. I like to take a long ruler and using a chalk pencil mark a line exactly in the center running N to S and then another line running E to W. This gives you a good reference point to make sure the motifs line up in the same place block to block. Referring to the quilt photo begin placing the cut out shapes onto

Fig. 5. Appliquéd block

the green background fabric. Make sure that the colors and placement are to your liking. Remember, it is not important that every piece be exactly placed. Once you have everything in place you can start the fusing process. Follow the manufacturer's instructions for the fusible you have chosen to use. It is often helpful to score the backing paper with a pin to help peel the paper more easily. Using a buttonhole stitch and matching thread stitch around all appliqué pieces in each block. Be sure to use a locking stitch at the beginning and ending of each stitching line.

That's it, your top is complete!

Completing the Quilt

Cut backing yardage into two (2) equal lengths, take time to trim selvages off the fabric before sewing the center seam. Piece backing sections together along the trimmed edge using a ¼" seam. Press seam to one side for security and strength. I like to leave the remaining selvages on the backing fabric for stability when loading and quilting the quilt. Layer the quilt top, batting and backing and quilt as you wish.

Binding

For binding preparation and application refer to the General Quiltmaking Instructions, p. 20.

Don't forget to label your quilt!

Quilt assembly, appliqué added after blocks are pieced

SEVILLE, 56" x 56". Designed and quilted by Linda Thielfoldt and pieced by Janet Rose. A bold and busy paisley print is the perfect fabric for this alternate version of SEVILLE. Fabrics in grays, blacks, and a light yellow really change up the look of this quilt. Linda quilted this in an all over paisley pattern which shows that not every quilt needs custom quilting.

Carnivale, 57" x 72"
Pieced and quilted by Linda Thielfoldt

CARNIVALE
· · · · · · · · · · · ·

Block Size: 12¾" x 12¾"

This quilt just says fun to me. The lively floral print; the fun string pieced triangles; the traditional appliqué motif done in bright colors on the pure white background all combine nicely to bring this happy quilt to life.

Materials and Fabrics Needed

Red Floral Print – 1¼ yards for large triangles

Lime Green Polka Dot – 1¼ yards for outer border

White – 1 yard for block backgrounds and sashing (tone-on-tone fabric)

Fat Quarters – 15 to 20 or equivalent scraps in several shades of green, blue, red, orange, yellow, turquoise and pink to be used for string blocks and floral appliqué

Stripe Fabric – ½ yard for binding

Backing – 4 yards your choice of fabric

Batting – twin size

Tissue Paper or Newsprint –
5 pieces for string piecing – 13" x 13" square
12 pieces for string piecing – 8" x 8" square

Fusible Web – 2 yards

> ### *Designer Tip*
> Before you cut up your fat quarters into strings it is a good idea to choose the fabrics for the appliqué and prepare the pieces. The strings can then be cut from the remaining fabric.

Quilt Components

This quilt is a little different than the rest of the quilts in the book due to the string piecing. You will be making two (2) different sized string "blocks" and once complete, those blocks will be cut into triangles and used to surround the appliqué blocks and also the triangle border. String piecing is fun and forgiving and don't be intimidated if you have never tried it before.

Cutting

String Blocks

You need to make some strings! Take the fat quarters and scraps you have gathered and start cutting them into strips or "strings" that vary in width from ¾" to 1½" by the WOF. The great thing about this is you don't have to cut a specific size, just make them straight. I don't like to use anything smaller than ¾" due to the seam allowance and by the same token anything bigger than 1½" is too wide and really stands out in the size blocks used in this quilt. Make sure you have a wide selection of color variation in your strings. You can't use too many fabrics in these blocks.

Appliqué Blocks
White Tone-on-Tone Print

(6) 9½" x 9½" squares

Your Fat Quarters or Scraps

(6) 4¼" x 4¼" squares

Sashing
White Tone-on-Tone Print

(7) 2" x WOF strips then cut the following sizes:

(3) 13¼" x 2"

(3)★ 27½" x 2"

(1)★ 30½" x 2"

(2)★ 41¾" x 2"

> ### Designer Tip
> ★You may want to wait to subcut these pieces until after your blocks are complete in case you have any variation in size and need to adjust the length a little.

Side and Corner Triangles
Red Floral Print

(2) 16" x 16" squares and then cut once on the diagonal for corner triangles

(3) 11⅜" x 11⅜" squares and then cut once on the diagonal for side triangles

Border
Lime Green Polka Dot

(6) 6½" x WOF strips

Binding
Stripe Print

(7) 2" x WOF strips cut on the straight of grain

> ### Note
> The binding strips were cut on the bias. Adjust your cutting if you choose to do the same.

Block Assembly

Appliqué

Trace all appliqué shapes onto the paper side of the fusible web using a mechanical pencil. Appliqué pattern is on p. 93. At this point you will have to decide on colors. Use the photo of the quilt as your guide. Cut out all the fusible pieces using paper scissors or snips, I opted to skip the Halo method described on p. 16 due to the size of the pieces. Fuse your fabrics and cut out. Make certain your stems extend past the drawing to allow for the overlap. This is very important since you will be adding the triangle at the bottom of each block.

Appliqué the Blocks

Start by finding the center of each white square. Referring to the quilt photo begin placing the cut out shapes onto the white tone-on-tone background fabric. Make sure that the colors and placement are to your liking. The stem must extend below the line where the triangle will be added. Remember, it is not important that every piece be exactly placed. Once you have everything in place you can start the fusing process. Follow the manufacturer's instructions for the fusible you have chosen to use. It is often helpful to score the backing paper with a pin to help peel the paper more easily. Using a buttonhole stitch and matching thread stitch around all appliqué pieces in each block. Be sure to use a locking stitch at the beginning and ending of each stitching line.

Once the appliqué is complete take the 4¼" x 4¼" turquoise squares and draw a line on the diagonal. Place the square on the lower corner of the block being sure to cover the end of the stem. Sew on the drawn line. Press the square toward the corner and trim away the extra layers leaving only a ¼" seam. Square up the corner if necessary.

Make the String Blocks

Take each square of tissue paper and fold in half down the middle, make a good crease you can see. Lay the first string on this line and lay another one directly on top. Sew along the edge using a ¼" seam allowance. Press. Continue adding strings until you have the paper covered. The strings should hang over the edge of the tissue paper on all sides.

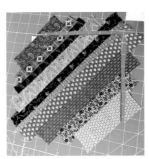

Make twelve (12) string blocks using the 8" x 8" tissue paper and five (5) string blocks using the 13" x 13" tissue paper.

When trimming up your string blocks place a square ruler on the diagonal seam of each block and trim making sure the first seam runs diagonally from corner to corner. This keeps everything straight.

Cut the smaller blocks to 6¾" x 6¾" and then cut on the diagonal <u>across</u> the strings.

Cut the larger blocks to 11⅜" x 11⅜" and then cut on the diagonal <u>across</u> the strings.

Add the smaller string triangles to each of the appliqué blocks.

Quilt Assembly

Begin by sewing the 2" x 13¾" sashing strips between the six (6) appliqué blocks in pairs of two (2) with the strips in the center.

Sew each set of two (2) blocks to a 2" x 27½" strip along the lower edge of each set of two (2). Sew the sets together leaving the top sashing strip for later. Sew the 2" x 41¼" sashing strips to each side and then finally add the top 2" x 30½" sashing strip. I constructed it this way to eliminate seams in the long sashing strips.

Layout the string triangles and the red floral print triangles as shown in the quilt assembly diagram. Sew together the five (5) triangles for each side and then add to the sides of the quilt. Press toward the red fabric. Sew together the three (3) top and bottom triangles and sew to both edges of the quilt. Press to the red fabric. Sew the larger red floral triangles on last and press toward the red.

Outer Border

Trim the ends off the border strips and sew end to end. Measure your quilt and starting with the top and bottom borders, cut a strip of border fabric to your exact measurements. Press to the green fabric. Measure the length of your quilt and cut two (2) more strips to your exact measurements. I always pin my borders at each end and then in the middle making certain everything is nice and flat before I sew. Since my print border reads as a solid it did not matter to me where the seams ended up. Adjust your border cuts according to your fabric. If you have a larger busy print you may want to fussy cut and piece your border strips.

Completing the Quilt

Cut backing yardage into two (2) equal lengths, take time to trim selvages off the fabric before sewing the center seam. Piece backing sections together along the trimmed edge using a ¼" seam. Press seam to one side for security and strength. I like to leave the remaining selvages on the backing fabric for stability when loading and quilting the quilt. Layer the quilt top, batting, and backing and quilt as you wish.

Binding

For binding preparation and application refer to the General Quiltmaking Instructions, p. 20.

Don't forget to label your quilt!

Quilt assembly

Patterns

· · · · · · · · · · ·

MIDNIGHT IN BALTIMORE

Block 1, Quilt p. 22

ENLARGE 400%

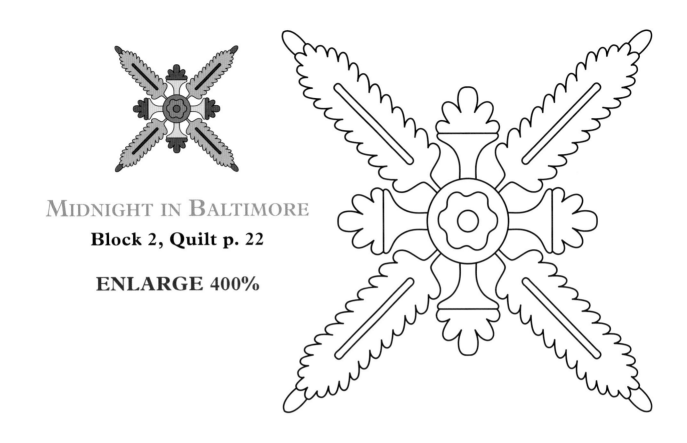

MIDNIGHT IN BALTIMORE

Block 2, Quilt p. 22

ENLARGE 400%

MIDNIGHT IN BALTIMORE

Block 3, Quilt p. 22

ENLARGE 400%

MIDNIGHT IN BALTIMORE

Block 4, Quilt p. 22

ENLARGE 400%

MIDNIGHT IN BALTIMORE

Block 5, Quilt p. 22

ENLARGE 400%

MIDNIGHT IN BALTIMORE

Block 6, Quilt p. 22

ENLARGE 400%

MIDNIGHT IN BALTIMORE

Block 7, Quilt p. 22

ENLARGE 400%

MIDNIGHT IN BALTIMORE

Block 8, Quilt p. 22

ENLARGE 400%

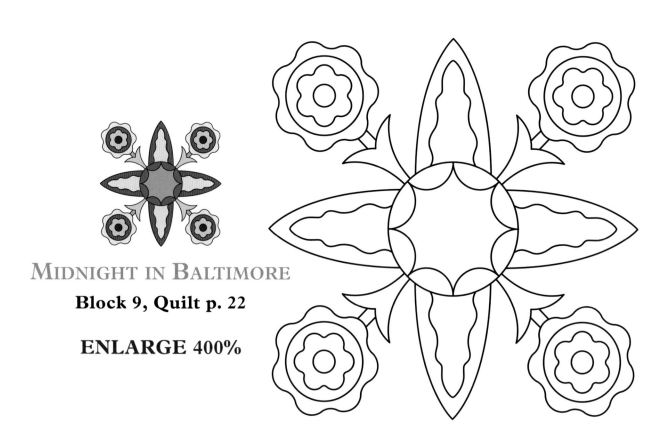

MIDNIGHT IN BALTIMORE

Block 9, Quilt p. 22

ENLARGE 400%

ON MY WAY TO BALTIMORE

Quilt p. 28

ENLARGE 400%

CHATHAM COUNTY
Quilt p. 34

ENLARGE 400%

RASPBERRY LIMEADE
Quilt p. 39

ENLARGE 400%

MARYLAND ROSE
Quilt p. 44

ENLARGE 400%

TULIP SPLENDOR

Quilt p. 51

ENLARGE 400%

PERKINS PURPLE PLUMES

Quilt p. 57

SHOWN at 100%

NOTTINGHAM POMEGRANATE
Quilt p. 63

ENLARGE 400%

SEVILLE
Quilt p. 70

ENLARGE 400%

CARNIVALE

Quilt p. 76

ENLARGE 200%

. . . . *Patterns*

Linda Thielfold ❀ *On My Way to* BALTIMORE   **93** ❀

About the Author

· · · · · · · · · · · ·

Linda Thielfoldt, owner of The Quilted Goose in her hometown of Troy, Michigan, has been quilting for over 40 years, teaching machine quilting for over 25 years, and loves to share her knowledge. Her classes are taught in a no-rules, fun, and lively style that provides inspiration and new ideas on how to improve your machine quilting. Linda travels the country teaching at major shows and guilds and she specializes in being fearless with your quilting. She offers a wide variety of classes from quilting, piecing, appliqué, and everything in between. Linda designs patterns for computerized quilting machines and her patterns are available in many formats through www. legacyquilting.com. In addition to designing quilts, Linda is a writer of all things quilting and her articles have appeared in *Threads Magazine*, *American Patchwork & Quilting*, *On Track Magazine*, *The Quilter*, *The Quilt Life*, and in 2012 she appeared on The Quilt Show with Ricky and Alex.

Linda has been recognized for her quilting, quiltmaking, and wearable art skills at major shows across the US, winning her first national show in 2002. She has won at AQS Quiltweek Paducah, MQX, MQS, HMQS, Mancuso Shows, Vermont Quilt Festival, and Road to California, to name a few, as well as many local and regional shows. She has won over 100 ribbons and several best of show and viewers' choice awards.

Feel free to reach out to her, on her blog:
http://lindathielfoldtthequiltedgoose.blogspot.com
on her Facebook page: www.facebook.com/
    TheQuiltedGoose
via her website: www.thequiltedgoose.com
or her email: info@thequiltedgoose.com

Linda's ribbon collection

OPPOSITE: Nottingham Pomegranate variation, full quilt on page 69.

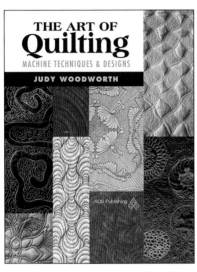

#11140

#10310

#10283

Enjoy these and more from AQS

AQS Publishing brings the latest in quilt topics to satisfy the traditional to modern quilter. Interesting techniques, vivid color, and clear directions make these books your one-stop for quilt design and instruction. With its leading Quilt-Fiction series, mystery, relationship, and community all merge as stories are pieced together to keep you spell-bound.

Whether Quilt-Instruction or Quilt-Fiction, pick one up from AQS today.

#10286

#10285

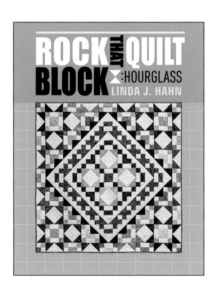

#10278

AQS publications are available nationwide.
Call or visit AQS
www.shopAQS.com
1-800-626-5420